Raglavar/Introduction

Penzance, Redruth, Bodmin, Launceston; Co
place-names. These names are considered strange because they are not English.
This should come as no surprise as 75% of Cornish place-names are derived, not from
English, but Cornish – the Celtic language of Cornwall. What is surprising to many is that
the Cornish language is not dead, like Latin, but very much alive and kicking. Personal
names are very much part of the language. To understand how these names came into
being you need to appreciate the fact that Cornish history is very different to that of her
larger neighbour to the East.

Tamm Istori Kernewek/A Bit of Cornish History

During the millennium celebrations, many papers and TV programmes looked back
at the last century. In 1900 there was no Cornish language! Nobody could speak,
write or even read Cornwall's Celtic language. So what happened?

To answer this fully you must realize that Cornwall has a unique history. Two millennia
ago Britain was populated by British tribes. When the Romans came, they found a
number of small kingdoms that spoke the British language and worshipped their gods
under a druidic priesthood. The Dumnonii, the Celtic kingdom occupying the Southwest
peninsula of Britain on the Western fringe of the Empire, was little influenced by the
Roman invasions. Exeter was a frontier town.

The invasion of Britain by Angles, Jutes and Saxons, coupled with a series of dreadful
plagues, caused mass migrations of Celts to Brittany. These immigrants mixed into the
native Gaulish Celtic population and so the nation of Brittany was founded. Meanwhile
back in Britain, the advance of the Saxons was halted by Arthur. Without his brilliant
military leadership perhaps there would be no Wales or Cornwall today.

At this time many holy men and women came from Brittany and Ireland and converted
the Celtic half of Britain to Christianity. Because Cornwall protrudes into the sea, it
became a centre of Celtic voyages and pilgrimage.

Shortly before the first millennium, Celtic people inhabited the Southwest of Britain in
what is today Cornwall and Devon. In 936 AD, the Saxon King Athelstan ethnically

cleansed the city of Exeter and Devon. He declared that 'the River Tamar shall be the border between my kingdom of Wessex and the kingdom of Cornwall', and so created the Celtic country of Cornwall. The word Cornwall is derived from two Saxon words. *Corn* means 'corner' and *wealas* 'foreigners, serfs, inferior people'. The second word also gave rise to Wales so like our Celtic cousins the Welsh, we are foreigners in own country! Many people therefore prefer to use the Cornish word for Cornwall – **Kernow**.

Saxons then started to colonize the eastern fringes of Cornwall. This was halted instantly when William the Conqueror invaded Britain. One third of William's army was not Norman but Breton, led by Alan of Brittany. It may have been because of this that Cornwall was kept as a single territorial unit and given to Mortain, William's half brother, a Breton. The Cornish-Breton relationship laid the foundations for centuries of peace allowing the development of the **Plen an Gwari** Culture. Religious plays with a strong local flavour were performed in amphitheatres, **plenyow an gwari,** across the whole of Cornwall.

1497 saw the Cornish rebel against the English crown. Henry VII had suspended the Cornish Stannary Parliament and the Cornish feared being ruled from London. Under the leadership of Michael Joseph, the blacksmith of **Lannaghevran**/St. Keverne and the **Bosvenegh**/Bodmin lawyer Thomas Flamank, some 20,000 Cornish marched 300 miles to London to take on the English. They were armed with bows, pikes and canon. After winning the Battle of Guildford, the Cornish met the English troops who had been mustered to invade Scotland. At Blackheath many of the Cornish fled and, after 1,000 had been killed, Joseph and Flamank surrendered to prevent further slaughter of their fellow countrymen. The war was finally resolved when The Cornish Stannary paid £1,000 to King Henry VII in 1508. In return the crown granted the Cornish the *Great Charter of Pardon* – enshrining the rights of the Stannary legal system – effectively letting the people of Cornwall govern themselves.

King Henry VIII was tolerant of the Cornish but, on his death, the boy king Edward was powerless to prevent a ruthless group of English lords seizing control. In 1549 an English language *Common Book of Prayer* was forced onto the **Kernewek**/Cornish speaking population. They rebelled, led by Sir Humphrey Arundell of **Hellann**/Helland near **Bosvenegh**/Bodmin. The city of Exeter was put under siege and this gave time for the English to hire foreign mercenaries, 450 Italian arquebusiers, 1,000 German Lanzkechts and 1,000 Welsh dragoons. The majority of the Cornish were not killed in battle but in a series of bloody massacres. 900 unarmed prisoners at Clyst, 1,000 Cornish captured and hung as they fled to Somerset and over a thousand Cornishmen were hung over the length and breadth of Cornwall by Sir Anthony Kingston and his death squads. One in nine of the Cornish population or every other man of breeding age was murdered. There is no record of the number of widows and orphans who died in the resultant famines as farms, mines and fisheries collapsed. The Cornish language was dealt a further blow when Glasney College and the Catholic Church were destroyed and Cornwall's links with her sister country Brittany were severed.

The Tamar is just as much a linguistic border as a geographical border. The Cornish rebellions of 1497 and 1549 led to the decimation of Cornish speaking communities. So running through Cornwall's history is Cornwall's language.

An Yeth Kernewek/The Cornish Language

The names in this book are from the Cornish language and her place amongst the Celtic languages is shown below.

	Brittonic (P-Celtic)	*Brezhoneg*, (Breton) *Cymraeg* (Welsh) **Kernewek** (Cornish)
Celtic languages		
	Goidelic (Q-Celtic)	*Gaeilge* (Irish) *Gaidhlig* (Scottish Gaelic) *Gaelg* (Manx)

Cornish grew out of the ancient British tongue spoken from **Penn an Wlas**/Lands End to the North of Scotland. **Lannergh**/Lanner in West and **Lannergh**/ Landrake in Southeast Cornwall are derived from the same British root as Lanark in Scotland. Even Pictish in the far North was a dialect of British. This language has gradually evolved into the three Brittonic languages. These form the P-Celtic branch of the Celtic family of languages that survive today.

The Saxon language then started to nibble away at the east of Cornwall. This process ceased when William the Conqueror arrived and made large land grants to the Bretons who had supported him. At about this time the *Vocabulum Cornicum*, a Latin – Cornish vocabulary was written, possibly to teach priests the Cornish language.

Old Cornish (800 to 1200) then gave way to Middle Cornish (1200 to 1575). Epic poetry such as *Passhyon Agan Arloedh* developed. Literature in Cornish blossomed further into the **Plen an Gwari** Culture. Great plays such as *Bywnans Meryasek* and **An Ordinali** were performed in outdoor amphitheatres. There is evidence of some 20 **plen an gwari** in Cornwall from east of **Lyskerrys**/Liskeard to **Lannyust**/St. Just in Penwith in the far west of the country.

Shortly before the bloody events of 1549, the Cornish army issued a list of articles against the imposition of the English Book of Common Prayer. One of the articles is as follows,

> "…we the Cornish, whereof certain of us understand no English, do utterly refuse the new [English language] service."

Cornish died as the language of the majority of Cornish people in 1549 and died as a community language, even in the far west around 1600. The Newlyn School bravely tried to halt the complete death of the language but the last monoglot, Chesten Marchant of **Sen Goedhyan**/Gwithian, died in 1676 and the last person able to write sentences of traditional Cornish was William Bodinar, who died in 1789.

The Revival is generally accepted as beginning with The *Handbook of the Cornish Language* by Henry Jenner, published in 1904. In the same year, Jenner made a speech in Cornish at Caernarfon, which finally convinced the other Celtic countries to admit Cornwall to the Celtic Congress. The Revival took another step forward when, in 1928, the first modern **Gorsedh Kernow**/Cornish Gorsedd was held at **Bosskawenn Woen**/Boscawen-Un near **Eglosveryan**/St. Buryan. Jenner was the first **Bardh Meur**/Grand Bard and truly earned the title 'Father of the Cornish Language Revival.'

Examinations in the Cornish language were started in 1962 and **Kesva an Taves Kernewek**/Cornish Language Board was set up in 1967 to administer the growing demand. **Kowethas an Yeth Kernewek**/Cornish Language Fellowship began in 1979 to support those who wished to make the language part of their everyday life.

The revived language is called **Kernewek** (the Cornish word for Cornish) and is used here to distinguish it from the various forms of Cornish dialect.

Ytho dhe'n dalleth an tressa milvlydhen, Kernewek yw unnweyth arta yeth vyw may hyll Kernow kavoes hy le gwiw y'n teylu a genedhlow Keltek.

(So at the beginning of the third millennium, **Kernewek** is once again a living language allowing **Kernow** to take her rightful place in the family of Celtic nations.)

HENWYN PERSONEK KERNEWEK/CORNISH PERSONAL NAMES

Personal names are a small but significant part of **Kernewek** and show the world that, with their use, the culture of Cornwall is very much alive. Many of the names are very ancient indeed. Some have their roots in the British language spoken across the whole of Britain in pre-Roman times. *Catu-uindos* is such a name, with the loss of the final syllables in the 5th or 6th century, it gave rise to Old Cornish *Cadwyn* and Old Welsh *Cadwin*. Around 1100, the middle <d> became <s> giving us Middle Cornish *Caswyn, *Kaswyn*. In modern spelling it becomes **Kaswynn** and as any Cornish speaker of today will tell you; the meaning of this name is 'fair battle'. Perhaps this would be a fitting name for a boisterous toddler or a nom de plume for a battling local councillor.

Nevet means 'sacred grove' from Gaulish and British but also found as a personal name in Old Welsh. It was cornicised to ***Neves** and then anglicised and combined with **karn** 'rock-pile' to give us the place-name Carnevas in St. Merryn parish in mid Cornwall. Why did this man settle in Cornwall and why was a carn named after him? The mystery remains embedded in the age of **Arthur** and the Saints but what a great story someone of that name could tell their friends.

Many names came from our sister country Brittany. *Seder* is an Old Breton name, meaning 'cheerful,' and was brought to Cornwall and gave rise to Tresidder near **Porthkernow**/Porthcurno in the west of the country. The place-name has also become a Cornish family-name. If the name Tresidder is to be lost through marriage why not give a child a name, like **Seder**, to preserve this remarkable Celtic link.

Some names originate from Cornwall such as Old Cornish *Wurci* giving us **Gorgi.** The meaning, 'super dog', may seem strange to us today but it must have been popular in the last millennium as it combined with **bos** 'dwelling', **kar** 'camp', **ynys** 'island, isolated place', **kelli** 'grove' and **tre** 'farm, settlement' to give Bosworgey, Carworgey, Ennisworgey, Killaworgey, Trevorgay, Treworgey and Treworgie.

Many names came from Ireland, Wales and Brittany during the Age of Saints. Holy men and women brought Christianity to Cornwall long before the pagan Saxons, Jutes and Angles were converted. Many names have fantastic stories associated with them such as **Ia** the Irish woman who sailed to Cornwall on a leaf! **Keyna**, daughter of King Brychan of Wales, has her holy well at St. Keyne in Southeast Cornwall. Newly wed couples visit this magical well and whoever is first to drink the water will be the dominant partner in the marriage. Perhaps the women of Cornwall should bestow the name of **Keyna** upon their daughters to ensure the continuation of female dominance in Cornish society!

The Making of Modern Europe tells of one church in Europe using one language, Latin. Personal names also were becoming uniform from Ireland to Central Europe.

> "By the later Middle Ages the process of homogenization in naming patterns had gone far. Of the fourteenth century councillors of Dresden, for example, over 30% bore the name of John, almost 24% the name Nicholas, over 15% Peter."

With the military dominance of the Normans in Britain this process affected the stock of Cornish names. **Jenefer** survived only in Cornwall but even **Arthur** and *Enid* as names were 19th century revivals. English names also suffered; Alfred and Edwina also being recent revivals.

In the Cornwall Military Survey of 1522, the vast majority of Christian names are common e.g. John, William, Thomas and Richard. Cornish forms of these names i.e. **Yowann**, **Wella** and **Tommos** are not found but **Hykka** is found as *Hecka*. However there are some distinctive names to be found and revived. **Paskow**, **Madern** and **Klemmens** are great names that were in use in 14th century Cornwall. Some names such as **Morven** and **Udin** were probably brought over from our sister country Brittany.

The Subsidies for Cornwall of 1525 and 1543 show a wider range of names but Christian names of Celtic origin are rare. However **Paskow** spelt *Pascoe, Pascoo, Pascow* and *Pasco*, meaning 'of Easter' and **Petrek** spelt *Petrok* and *Petrock* are found all over the country – even the then English speaking areas. There was a *Pascoe Bere* of **Lannaled**/St. Germans and a *Petrok Glovyer* of **Essa**/Saltash. Again people such as *Morveth Bretton age 16, servant* are classed as 'alien'. **Kernewek** and Breton (Brezhoneg) were so similar that many Bretons came to live in **Kernow**/Cornwall. In some southern parishes, up to 20% of the population was Breton born and were recorded as 'aliens'. This exchange was halted with the Prayer Book Wars of 1549.

Some Cornish names are equivalents for names in use today. After **Kernewek** died as a community language around 1600, some revivalists used these equivalents. William Rowe of Sancreed lived in the 17th century and translated parts of the Bible into

Kernewek. He signed himself as **Wella Rowe**. Today the prolific Cornish language writer **Jowann Richards** uses the Cornish version of John. Joy Stevenson, the Cornish dialect expert, wrote a magazine column under the name Maid **Lowena**, **Lowena** being the Cornish for Joy. There is a short list of Cornish equivalents at the end of this book if you need a *nom de plume* or wish to cornicise your own name.

Although **Gorsedhow** in Cornwall are mentioned in the ancient tales of *Y Mabinogi*, the first modern **Gorsedh Kernow**/Cornish Gorsedd was held in 1928. When a person becomes a bard of **Gorsedh Kernow**, the greatest honour that our country can bestow, they must choose a bardic name, which is of course, in the Cornish language. Since the first modern **Gorsedh**/Gorsedd, a small number of very attractive names have been coined. **Kerghydh** 'heron' is the bardic name of **Wella Herring**, the first person to teach the Cornish language as part of the school curriculum. **Gwennel** 'swallow' is the bardic name of **Sue Smith** who helped found **Dalleth** – the children's group.

Many fine names can be culled from the modern dictionaries. However it would be good to check the meanings beforehand. **Gwynngala** is a good sounding name and means 'September'. **Sevienn** is Cornish for 'strawberry' and has a lovely sound to it and, to a Cornish speaker, would conjure up images of the sweet, scarlet fruit and long, hot summers.

To make up the deficiency of feminine names many can be constructed by use of the suffix **–a**. **Stefan**, the Cornish form of Stephen, can be feminized to **Stefana**, giving us a Cornish version of Stephanie; **Bernesa** for Bernardette and **Rabasa** for Roberta are constructed in this way. However lovely sounding feminine names such as **Dewina**, **Lybyana** and **Morvena** have no English equivalents.

Simply using Cornish spelling can renew many existing names. How about **Pegi**, **Judi** or **Karol** for girls and **Harri** and **Kolin** for boys? This practice is common in other Celtic languages and means that you don't even need to change how your name is pronounced.

Lytherennans/Spelling

A quick look at this book, or indeed a good dictionary, will show that **Kernewek** is not English and some of the letters are missing – shock horror! In the standard form of the language c, q, x or z are not found.

The strangest omission (to the monoglot English speaker) is that of the letter <c>. If you look at modern Welsh there is no letter <k>. The Welsh language uses <c>. If you look at the language of Brittany, we see that there is no letter <c> the Bretons use <k>. Only the English language has a weird and wonderful mixture of <c> and <k> that bedevils both the dyslexic and the logical.

Kernewek, like Welsh but unlike English, distinguishes in writing the sound /θ/ written <th> and the sound /ð/ written <dh>. Bice in his book *Names For The Cornish,* says of the name Gorthelyk, Pron. "gawr-THEL-ik" with the "th" soft as in "then." Rather than spell the names as if in English and then have to explain each one I have spelt them as if they were Cornish words – which indeed they are. So Gorthelyk becomes **Gordhelyk**. The <dh> in Cornish corresponds to the Welsh <dd> and is a soft English <th> as in 'thy' but not the hard <th> as in 'thigh.'

Kernewek Kemmyn, the standard form of Cornish, is very nearly phonemic, that is to say that one letter, or pair of letters, has just one sound. Thus <g> is always hard as in 'get'. The soft sound written <g>, as in 'giant,' is provided by <j>. Once a few non-English sounds written as <oe> and <gh> are mastered, anyone can pronounce any word – and for that matter learn **Kernewek** really quickly.

Ledyans Lavaryans/Pronunciation Guide

Kernewek is very different from both English and Cornish dialect, but to someone without either, **Kernewek** is far easier to pronounce. It is possible to write a whole book on how to pronounce the language – indeed some people already have. A few simple guidelines here will help the monoglot English speaker make a reasonable stab at any of the names.

<dh> is always soft like <th> in English "this" and the place-name "Trewithen"

<g> is always hard like <g> in English "get" and the place-name "Germoe"

<gh> when at the end of a word is like <ch> Scottish "loch". When in the middle of word it becomes a heavy <h> like in the place-name "Portbyhan"

<i> is always like <i> in English "taxi"

<j> is always like <j> in English "jam" or the place-name "Jacobstow"

<oe> is one sound (it is not broken like bo-at) and found as <oa> in Cornish dialect "boat"

<ow> is like <ow> in English "grow" and like the <ow> in **Kernow**

<th> is always hard like <th> in English "think" or the place-name "Portreath"

<y> when followed by a consonant is like <y> in English "system" and the place-name "Harlyn." When followed by a vowel <y> is as in English "yank" or the place-name "Yellow Carn"

If you have any further questions or just want to make absolutely sure about something give the **Kowethas** a call on (01726) 882681.

POESANS/STRESS

Celtic languages, including **Kernewek**, usually carry the stress on the penultimate syllable. Don't worry about it as a Cornish accent takes care of this naturally. Two boys I grew up with in **Trewoen**/Troon were Anthony Penberthy and Anthony Pengelly. They were also known as Berthy and Gelly – showing that the first syllable of their surname was unstressed. In rapid dialect speech they became Berth and Gell. This clearly shows that it is the penultimate syllable is the one that is stressed, pen-BERTH-y and pen-GELL-y.

BERRHEANS HA FENTYNYOW/ABBREVIATIONS AND FONTS

m.   masculine name.

f.   feminine name.

OB   Old Breton 800 to 1100 AD
OC   Old Cornish 800 to 1200 AD
OW   Old Welsh 775 to 1150 AD

All words in **Kernewek** (the Cornish language) are printed in bold including the names. Place-names are given in their bilingual forms, Cornish first in bold followed by their modern map names e.g. **Bosvenegh**/Bodmin and **Aberfal**/Falmouth. Personal names and place-names in English, Welsh, Breton, Irish or French are not printed in bold e.g. Peter, Fychan, Arzher, Clodagh and Antoine. Quotes from historical sources are given in italic e.g. *Agnes Lannargh*. Forms in the British language are given in italic with a star to show that the form is not found but quoted (from Bice and Gover) e.g. *uindos saglos*.

This is not meant to be an academically rigorous study of Cornish Celtic names, merely a call to the people of Cornwall to celebrate the fact that we have a rich linguistic culture that includes the 1000 names featured here. Whilst I have taken care in compiling this list, especially in avoiding anglicisms, I am wholly responsible for the many inconsistencies and errors which have no doubt crept in.

So, with names from British, Breton, Welsh, our own Cornish saints, bards and our ever-growing language the choice for those who want a Cornish name for their children, to invent characters for stories or find a nom de plume for themselves is vast and varied.

Ytho, deun yn rag ha devnydhya agan yeth kernewek.

Pol Hodge
(Mab Stenek Veur)
Fentenwynn 2001

Adwen f.

This is an older form of **Aswen**. See **Aswen**.

Aghevran m.

This saint's name is remembered with the village of **Lannaghevran**/St. Keverne, on the Lizard peninsula. St. Just was accused of stealing **Aghevran's** communion plate and only gave the plate back when **Aghevran** threw great boulders at him. These can still be seen on Tremenheverne Downs meaning 'farm of St. Aghevran's stones'. See **Kevern**.

Agnes f.

Although not of Cornish origin this name is found in Cornish mythology. **Agnes** tricked giant Bolster into killing himself and so **Breannek** was changed to St. Agnes. In the Cornwall Military Survey of 1522 there is an *Agnes Lannargh* of **Eglosvadern**/Madron. **Lannergh** 'clearing' has given rise to Lanner and Landrake in Cornwall and Lannark in Scotland where the British language was spoken.

Alan m.

Equivalent of Breton Alan, Welsh Alun and French Alain. A saint of this name, originally from Wales, became bishop of Kemper/Quimper in Brittany and gave his name to **Sen Alan**/St. Allen, just north of **Truru**/Truro. A third of William the Conqueror's army consisted of Bretons led by **Alan** of Brittany.

Alban f.

This name in **Kernewek** means 'Scotland'.

Albers m.

A Cornish equivalent to Breton Alberz and English Albert.

Aldrydh m.

This is the Cornish version of the Welsh name Ardrydd. **Aldrydh** was a 8th century Celtic King of Herefordshire.

Alis f.

This is a Cornish equivalent of Breton Alis and English Alice.

Alson f.

In the Cornwall Military Survey of 1522 there is an *Alson Glyne* recorded as living in the parish of Stratton and an *Alson Nyclys* of **Kammbronn**/Camborne. The name is most likely a Cornish pet form of Alison and may be related to **Alsyn**.

Alsyn f.

Also from the Cornwall Military Survey of 1522 there is an *Alsyn Skelton* recorded as living in the borough of **Lannstefan**/Launceston. See also **Alson**.

Alusen f.

This name in **Kernewek** means 'charity'.

Alwar m.

He was a Cornish king in **Bywnans Meryasek**. **Alwar** may be an English name as found in Alverton, *Alwarton* in 1229. See **Meryasek**.

Amlodh m.

This was the name of the grandfather of **Arthur**.

Amon m.

He was **Amon** of Dyfed, father of S. Samson. See **Samson**.

Amys m.

In the Cornwall Military Survey of 1522 there is an *Amys Stabba* recorded as living in **Porthynys**/Mousehole in West Cornwall.

Androw m.

This a Cornish equivalent of the Breton Andrev, French André and English Andrew. A spelling of the family-name Andrew is found in the Cornwall Military Survey of 1522, *John Androw* of **Sen Menvre**/St. Minver Parish. See also **Androwa**.

Androwa f.

A feminine form of the above name and also an equivalent to the English Andrea See **Androw**.

Anna f.

She was Anna of Gwent, mother of **Sen Samson**. In Brittany, a pardon, or religious festival, is held in honour of S. Anna, mother of Mary. See **Samson**.

Annek m.

This mysterious name is found combined with **bre** 'hill' in **Breannek**, the Cornish name for St Agnes.

Annen m.

From OW this name is found in the place-name Bodannon.

Annik f.

This is a Cornish equivalent of Breton Annaig and English Annie. **Annik** makes use of the diminutive suffix **–ik**.

Annys f.

The Cornwall Subsidies record this name as *Annys Joce* of **Sen Sennen**/Sennen and *Annys Rawlyn wid.* of **Egloserm**/St. Eme in 1545.

Anoeth m.

In the triad of *The Three Very Famous Prisoners of the Island of Britain* **Anoeth** was a jailer.

Anson m.

This name is from OB and found in the place-name Trevanson. **Anson** is the Cornish equivalent of Breton Anton and French Antoine.

Anta f.

A saint's name found at **Lannanta**/Lelant, near **Heyl**/Hayle. The place-name is derived from **lann** 'holy site' + **Anta**.

Arghans f.

In **Kernewek** means 'silver'. This was a popular girls' name in 17th century Cornwall.

Arthega f.

A Cornish feminine form of the name below.

Arthek m.

This name is from OW and may be found in Trevarrack in St. Austell parish. The place-name may be derived from **ardhek** 'lofty' and means 'bear like'. The Welsh version is Arthog. See also **Arthega**.

Arthen m.

A Cornish version of the Welsh name Arthen. **Arthen** was a King of Ceredigan in the 9th century.

Arthur m.

He was, in fact, a real historical figure. **Arthur** was not a king but a brilliant military leader who led the British to 13 victories against the Saxons. The root of the name comes from **ors** – 'bear' and corresponds to the Breton Arzher. The name survived in Cornwall into Middle Ages. In the Cornwall Military Survey of 1522 there is an *Arthur Trevanters* of Warleggan and an *Arthur Kemys* of St. Kew. **Nyns yw marow Myghtern Arthur** translates as 'King Arthur is not dead!' and is a Gorsedd cry. It is believed by some that he was turned into a chough and will return to save the British from foreign invaders.

Arthvel m.

This name is a Cornish equivalent for the Breton Arzhel and means 'bear prince'. See also **Arthvela**.

Arthvela f.

A feminine form of the above name.

Arthyen m.

From OC and found in the place-name Trevarthian. It originally came from the British *arctogenos and means 'bear born'.

Aswen f.

She was one of the 24 children of King Brychan of Wales. This remarkable family went on to found churches all over the Celtic world. **Adwen,** an older form, is honoured at Advent at **Ryskammel**/Camelford. She is the Cornish patron of sweethearts – a sort of female St. Valentine. See also **Athwenna** and **Adwen**.

Attevell m.

The Cornwall Subsidies record this name as *Attevell Kerver* of the Borough of **Truru**/Truro in 1545.

Avarn m.

This name is found in the Cornish place-name of Bosavern < **bos** 'dwelling' + **Avarn**.

Avys m.

The Cornwall Subsidies record this name as *Avys Ford* of **Eglosheyl**/Eglosheyle Parish in 1545.

Awel f

This is the Cornish version of the Welsh name Awel which means 'breeze' in Welsh but **awel** is 'gale' in **Kernewek**. Perhaps this would make a good, if not tongue in cheek, equivalent for the English Gail or Gayle.

Awen f.

In **Kernewek** this name means 'muse, inspiration'. The same name also exists in Breton.

Awenek f.

This name in **Kernewek** means 'inspirational'.

Banadhlenn f.
This name from **Kernewek** means 'broom flower'.

Barennwynn f.
This newly created name means 'white, fair branch'.

Bastyan m.
A Cornish pet form of Sebastian. In 1522 there is a *Bastian Beesowe* recorded as *Bestyan Besaw* in 1543 from the parish of **Eglosvrega**/Breage.

Bekka f.
This name is found in the place-name Trevecca, a part of **Lyskerrys**/Liskeard and is a Cornish pet form of Rebecca.

Bennath f.
This modern name has the meaning 'blessing'.

Bennesik m.
Found in the early tenth century Bodmin Manumissions and means 'blessed'. This OC name might be found in the place-name Trenethick.

Berkla m.
The Cornwall Subsidies record this name as *Berkla William* of **Gwydhyel**/Withiel Parish in 1545. This name may be found in the place-name **Shoppaberkla**/Barcla Shop.

Bernes m.
This is the Cornish equivalent to Breton Bernez and the English Bernard. See also **Bernesa**.

Bernesa f.

A feminine form of the above name and so an equivalent for the French Bernardette.

Berran m.

This name is from OB and found in the place-name Trevarran in **Sen Kolomm**/St. Colomb.

Berthus m.

In the Cornwall Military Survey of 1522 there is a *Berthus Polye* recorded as living in the parish of **Logsulyen**/Luxulyan.

Beryl f.

Equivalent of English Beryl.

Berwynn m.

This name is from OW and found in the place-name Treverren. See also **Berwynna**.

Berwynna f.

A Cornish feminine form of the above name.

Beryan f.

She was the daughter of an Irish chieften who came to Cornwall in the 5th century. **Beryan** is honoured at **Eglosveryan**/St. Buryan near **Pennsans**/Penzance and also has her name remembered in the English form of **Elerghi**/Veryan. King **Gerens** had his son cured of paralysis by prayers to St. Beryan. Her feast day is the 1st of May.

Besever m.

This is a Cornish form of Bedievere adopted here as he was one of the knights of **Arthur**. He threw **Kalespolgh** (Excalibur) into Dozmary Pool on Bodmin Moor.

Beskan m.

This name is from OB and found in the place-name Trevescan.

Besow m.

This is the **Kernewek** for Bissoe near **Truru**/Truro which simply means 'birch trees'. **Besow** is also the Cornish version of the Welsh name Bedwyn.

Besowenn f.

This is **Kernewek** for 'a birch tree'. All single trees are feminine in **Kernewek**.

Berrwynn m.

A Cornish version of the Welsh name Berwyn. **Berrwynn** means 'white mound'.

Berrwynna f.

This is the feminine version of the Welsh masculine name Berwyn.

Betti f.

From the derivative of English Elizabeth and used in Welsh.

Bettsi f.

From the derivative of English Elizabeth and respelled in Cornish.

Bili m.

This name is from OB and found in the place-name Carbilly.

Bleujenn f.

In **Kernewek** this name means 'flower' and is the equivalent to Breton Bleuñvenn and French Flore. **Bleujenn** was a character in **Denladh dhe'n Orsedh** by **Polin Preece**.

Melhes:	Go-ev, go-ev! Marow yw an Bardh Meur!	Poor him, poor him! Dead is the Grand Bard!
Bleujenn:	Marow! Go-ev, go-ev!	Dead! Poor him, poor him!
Elester:	Mes pandr'a hwarva?	But what happened?
	Fatell yll bos marow?	How can he be dead?
	Yowynk ha yagh o ev!	Young and healthy was he!

Blewek m.

This nick name in **Kernewek** means 'hairy'.

Bleydh m.

This name is found in the place-name Trembleath and means 'wolf'. It also corresponds to the Breton name Bleiz.

Bleydhik m.

An eqivalent name that is attested in OW and is found in the place-name Tremblethick and means 'little wolf'.

Bleydhri m.

An equivilent name found in OW and in the place-name Tremblary and means 'wolf king'.

Bodhenn f.

From **Kernewek** this name means 'corn marigold'.

Bonnik f.

This name in **Kernewek** means 'meadow pipit'.

Borlewen f.

From OW this name is found in the place-name Bodannon and in **Kernewek** means 'morning star, Venus'. **Borlewen** is the name of the home of Cornish language bard and artist **June Luxton**.

Bowdyn m.

In the Cornwall Military Survey of 1522 there is a *Bowdyn sevant of Thomas Kenegy* recorded as living in the parish of **Sen Germogh**/Germoe.

Bran m.

This name is found in the place-name Bodbrane. Today **bran** also means 'crow, raven' the sacred bird of the ancient Celts that pecked out the eyes of dead warriors so that they would not see the way to **Annown** – the other world.

Branega f.

A feminine form of the name below.

Branek m.

From both OB and OW and is found in the place-name Trennack. See also **Branega**.

Branwalader m.

This saint's name is found at **Sen Branwalader**/St. Breward, near **Bosvenegh**/Bodmin. **Branwalader** means 'raven leader'. His feast day is 19th of January.

Brathagh m.

This name is from OW and found in the place-name Trembothack.

Brega f.

She came from Ireland and established her church at **Eglosvrega**/Breage near **Hellys**/Helston.

Brengi m.

This name is found in the early tenth century Bodmin Manumissions and means 'noble hound'. **Brengi** is from OW and found in the place-name Trefingey.

Briallenn f.

In **Kernewek** meaning 'primrose'. The bardic name of **Ann Trevenen Jenkin**, the first woman Grand Bard, is based on this name.

Briek m.

He was born in Wales and came to Cornwall in the 6th century. Briek founded the church at **Nanssans**/St. Breock, near **Ponsrys**/Wadebridge. His feast day is 1st May. The place-name Trevigue may also contain this OB name.

Brisgi m.

This name is found in the place-name Treviskey.

Brithel m.

From OC and found in the place-name Ponsbrital combined with **pons** 'bridge'.

Brithennek m.

The name means 'speckled, freckled' and was the bardic name of **Brian Webb**. He was the first secretary of **Kowethas an Yeth Kernewek** and wrote and performed many fine songs in **Kernewek** that are still sung by the **kernewegoryon** today.

Bronndeg f.

This name in modern **Kernewek** means 'fair, white breast'.

Bronnwynn f.

A Cornish equivalent of the Welsh Bronwen and means 'fair breast'.

Bryvyth m.

This saint founded the church at **Lannlivri**/Lanlivery near **Bosvenegh**/Bodmin.

Budhek m.

Equivalent of English Victor or Vic and found at Budock Water, near **Aberfal**/Falmouth. He was born in a barrel when his Breton mother, Azenor, was cast into the sea after being wrongly accused of adultery. **Budhek** himself floated back to Brittany in a stone coffin. He founded a church at **Plywvudhek**/Budock, near **Aberfal**/Falmouth and at St. Budeaux in **Aberplymm**/Plymouth. His feast day is 8th December. This OC name is also found in the place-names Trebithick and Trevithick. This gave rise to the family name of Richard Trevithick who invented the car as well as the steam locomotive.

Budhega f.

Cornish form of Boadicea, Queen of the Isceni, who fought the Romans, burned London and finally poisoned herself rather than be taken prisoner – a typical Celtic woman!

Bulugenn f.

A name in **Kernewek** means 'worm'. The Cornish dialect word belugan means 'small child'.

Byghan m.

A name is from OW and found in the place-name Trebiffin and means 'little'.

Byw m.

This name is found in the place-name Lesbew and means 'lively'.

Bywega f.

A feminine form of the name below.

Bywek m.

Another name is from OW and might be found in the place-name Trebreak and means 'abounding in life'. See also **Bywega**.

Bywgi m.

This name is from OW and found in the place-name Trevigo and means 'lively dog'.

Chesten f.

This is a Cornish version of the English Christine. **Chesten Marchant** of **Sen Goedhyan**/Gwithian was reputedly the last monoglot speaker of the Cornish language. She died in 1676.

Chigokk f.

This name in modern **Kernewek** means 'house martin'.

Danek m.

This name is from OW and found in the place-name Tredannick.

Davi m.

Equivalent of English Davy and Welsh Dafi.

Davydh m.

Another equivalent of English David, Welsh Dafydd.

Day m.

He is, of course, honoured at St. Day near **Rysrudh**/Redruth. Older people of this parish still use the older, and more correct, pronunciation i.e. to rhyme with 'cry'. There is also a St. Dei in Brittany.

Degi m.

This name is found in the place-names of Tregithey and Trethiggey.

Degymman m.

This name appears on the modern map as Degibna near **Hellys**/Helston.

Delega f.

A feminine form of the name below.

Delek m.

He was one of the 24 children of King Brychan of Wales. This remarkable family then founded churches all over the Celtic world. He is honoured at Port Isaac and there is a St. Illec in Brittany. See also **Delega**.

Delenn f.

This pretty name in **Kernewek** means 'leaf'.

Delennik f.

This name means 'little leaf' and is derived from **delenn** 'leaf' and **–ik** meaning 'little'.

Demelsa f.

A character in Poldark. The name is actually from Demelza the place-name of St. Wenn parish which is derived from **din** 'hill-fort' + **Melsa** 'a personal name'. This was written *Dynmalsa* in 1342.

Denys m.

This is the Cornish form of Breton Denez and English Dennis. **Dinas**/St. Dennis in mid Cornwall is actually derived from **dinas** meaning 'hill-fort'. However the patron saint of the church is St. Denys of Paris, a third century martyr. The place-name was *Seynt Denys* in 1436. See also **Denysa**.

Denysa f.

This is a Cornish equivalent of Breton Deneza and French and English Denise. See also **Denys**.

Derow m.

This strong name from **Kernewek** means 'oak'.

Dervow m.

This name is from OW and found in the place-name Trethuffe.

Derwa f.

This is found in the place-name Mendarva derived from **men** 'stone' + **Derwa**, near **Kammbronn**/Camborne.

Derwenn f.

Another name in modern **Kernewek** meaning 'oak tree'.

Dewi m.

This an OC name and equivalent of Welsh and Breton Dewi. He is honoured at **Lanndhewi**/Davidstow in North Cornwall. He is the patron saint of Wales and his feast day, Dydd Dewi Sant, is 1st March. This name is also found in the place-names Trethewy and Trethewey. **Dewi Annear** is a language bard and computer expert.

Dewin m.

From OW and found in the place-name Trethowan. See also **Dewina**.

Dewina f.

A feminine form of the above name. Remember the stress falls on the middle syllable; dew-IN-a.

Dinan m.

He was a local chieftain who built **Ia**'s church at **Porthia**/St. Ives. See **Ia**.

Diwel m.

This name is from OW and found in the place-name Boduel.

Dogho m.

The name survives in **Lanndhogo** the Cornish name for St. Kew.

Domina f.

In the Cornwall Military Survey of 1522 there is a *Domina Joan Arundell* recorded as living in the parish of **Sen Felek**/Phillack.

Donyerth m.

A Cornish version of the name found on the famous stone raised in his honour. It reads "Doniert Rogauit Pro Anima", and roughly translates as '**Donyerth** ordered this stone for the good of his soul'.

Dornell m.

This name is found in the place-name Boturnell. See also **Dornella**.

Dornella f.

A Cornish feminine form of the above name.

Drian m.

Found in both OB and OW and also in the place-name Bodrean. It rhymes with the name Ian.

Duan m.

This name is found in the place-name Trethuan.

Dyenn f.

From **Gerlyver Meur** and in **Kernewek** means 'cream'.

Dyjynn m.

This name in **Kernewek** means 'little piece'.

Dylan m.

From OW and found in Cornwall in the place-name Trethellan. Dylan Eil Don, meaning 'akin to wave' in Welsh was the name of a sea god. **Dylan Thomas** was a great English language poet from Wales.

Dyvan m.

This name is from OW and found in the place-name Trethevan.

Dywana f.

She was a legendary female ruler of Cornwall.

Ebon m.

This name is found in the place-name Trevibban.

Ebrenn f.

From **Kernewek** this is a bit of a hippy name meaning 'sky'.

Ebryl f.

An equivalent to the English name April. The month of April is strictly **mis-Ebryl**.

Ebrylwynna m.

This is the Cornish version of the Welsh name Ebrillwen and means 'white, fair April'.

Ebwynn m.

This mysterious name may be found in the place-name Carnebone and seems to contain the element **gwynn** 'white'.

Edern m.

Latin *Aeternus* gave rise to this name which is found in the place-name Treveddon. The Breton form of this name is also Edern. **Edern** is featured in the children's book **Diskudhans Edern**.

Egin m.

This name in **Kernewek** means 'sprout'.

Eginik m.

Using the suffix **–ik Egin** now becomes **Eginik** 'little sprout'.

Eleder m.

With an OW cognate this name is found in the place-name Trevillador.

Elek m.

This name is from OW and found in the place-name Bodellick.

Elena f.

A modern Cornish equivalent of Breton Elena or Lena and French Hélène.

Elester f.

This is a collective noun and so can be masculine or feminine. However **Elester** was a character in **Denladh an Orsedh** by **Polin Preece** and so the name is given here as feminine.

Jenkin:	Ha ple'ma y vyrgh, ytho?	And where is his daughter then?
	Gwreg an Bardh Meur?	Wife of the Grand Bard?
Elester:	Hi? Ogh, marow yw hi	She? Oh, she is dead
	Nans yw deg blydhen.	Ten years ago.
Jenkin:	Anfeusik yns, an teylu na,	They are unlucky that family,
	Dell hevel dhymm.	As it seems to me.
Elester:	Anfeusik mes meur aga	Unlucky but great their money!
	arghans!	

Elestrenn f.

This name in **Kernewek** means 'iris' and so is an equivalent to Iris.

Elik f.

Another sweet sounding name from **Kernewek** that uses the suffix **–ik** 'little'. **Elik** means 'cherub' or 'little angel'.

Elowenn f.

This beautiful name in **Kernewek** means 'elm-tree' and has been used as a bardic name as well.

Elvenn f.

In **Kernewek** this name means 'spark, element'.

Elvos m.

This name is from OW and found in the place-name Trevilvas.

Elwoes m.

From OW and found in the place-name Bodelva – the site of the Eden Project. What would **Elwoes**, the pioneer farmer, think of plants grown today at **Boselwoes**/Bodelva?

Elwynn m.

A Celtic saint came from Ireland in the 5th Century and founded a chapel at Pothleven, near **Hellys**/Helston. His life story was kept at **Eglosvrega**/Breage in 1538 but unfortunately did not survive.

Elyan m.

In the Cornwall Military Survey of 1522 there is an *Aelyan Toker* recorded as living in the parish of **Nansgwydhenn**/Lawitton.

Elys f.

In the Cornwall Subsidies for 1524 an *Eliz Tremayn wid.* recorded as living in the Borough of **Hellys**/Helston. This is a Cornish pet form of Elizabeth. See also **Eppow**.

Endelyn f.

She was one of the 24 children of King Brychan of Wales. This remarkable family went on to found churches all over the Celtic world such as St. Endellion near **Ponsrys**/Wadebridge. Her feast day is 29th of April.

Enni f.

The Irish name Clodagh, or Clóda in Irish, is derived from a river. In a similar way this name is derived from the Cornish river Inney which has the meaning 'river of ash trees'.

Enoder m.

Another Celtic saint who has his church at **Eglosenoder**/St. Enoder in Mid Cornwall. Bice says, "there are several records of the use of **Enoder** as a Christian name".

Enor f.

This is Cornish version of Breton Enora, Welsh Ynyr, French Honorée and American Honor.

Enosek m.

His church is situated on the banks of the Camel Estuary, near **Lannwedhenek**/Padstow.

Ensenin m.

According to Padel this name is found in the Cornish place-name Lantinning.

Enyen m.

OW gave rise to this name and it is found in the place-name Trevanion. **Denis Trevanion** was the **Bardh Meur Gorsedh Kernow**/Grand Bard of the Gorsedd of Cornwall 1970-1976. See also **Enyena**.

Enyena f.

A feminine form of the above name.

Enyon m.

This name is an equivalent to the Latin Annianus. **Enyon** was a legendary ruler of Cornwall.

Eos f.

In **Kernewek** means 'nightingale'. It is pronounced; E-os, with two syllables.

Eosik f.

This name in **Kernewek** means 'little nightingale'.

Eppow f.

A rare 16th century Cornish name is a Cornish pet form for Elizabeth corresponding to Betty, Beth, etc. See also **Elys**.

Erbin m.

This name is from OW and found in the place-name Treverbyn. Erbin is believed to be the father of St. Selevan. See also **Erbina**.

Erbina f.

A Cornish feminine form of the above name. With the stress on the middle syllable **Erbina** rhymes with 'carabina'.

Erghik m.

This name in **Kernewek** means 'snowy'. **Erghik** was the cat featured in the **Dres an Vlydhen** stories by **Brian Webb**.

Erghwynn f.

This name was derived as an equivalent for Snow White in the play and video **Erghwynn ha Peswar Stenor**, 'Erghwynn and the four tinners' by **Martyn Miller**.

Erghwynn:	Gorthugher da, dewgh a-ji.	Good evening, come inside.
	Esedhewgh orth an voes ha	Sit down at the table and
	Dalleth a wren. Te a vydh parys	We'll start. Tea will be
	Yn skon.	Ready soon.
Boss:	Hedh mynysenn kyns dalleth dybri.	Stop a minute before eating
	Yma hwans dhymm a neb derivas,	I want some meaning
	Po ni a wra leverel avel Norman	or we will say, like Norman
	Tebbit, 'on yer bike!'	Tebbit, 'on yer bike!'

Eriga m.

This is the femine form of **Erik** and so an equivalent to Erica.

Erik m.

A Cornish equivalent to Breton Erig and French Eric. See also **Eriga**.

Erk m.

He was an Irish bishop who landed at **Heyl**/Hayle and founded the church at **Lannudhno**/St. Erth.

Erthgi m.

This name is from OW and found in the place-name Bodargie.

Erven m.

His name survives in the village of **Sen Erven**/St. Ervan.

Esbell f.

The Cornwall Subsidies record this name as *Esbell Hoskyn* of Truro Borough in 1543. This is a Cornish pet form of Isabell, compare with Ishbel the Scottish Gaelic version of Isabell.

Eselda f.
Another older form of **Esels**, this time with the feminine suffix **-a**. See **Esels**.

Esels f.
This is Cornish version of the ancient name Ysolt. She, with her lover **Tristan**, fled from King **Margh** of Cornwall. They escaped the king's soldiers by wading across the Tresillian River at **Kammdrog**/Malpas See **Eselt**, **Eselda** and **Tristan**.

Eselt f.
Equivalent of Welsh Esyllt. See **Esels**.

Est m.
This name is from OC and might be found in the place-name Laneast. **Mis-Est** is the **Kernewek** for August.

Eudan m.
OB gave rise to this name that is found in the place-name Bosowa.

Euri m.
This name is from OW and may be found in the place-name Treverry.

Eva f.
This is a Cornish version found in Middle Cornish texts of Eve, Adam's wife in the Bible.

Eval m.
This name may be derived from Latin humilis from which our word **uvel** 'humble' comes.

Evan m.
In the Cornwall Subsidies for 1524 an *Evan Britton* is recorded as living in **Sen Pawl**/Paul.

Ewa f.
She is remembered at **Lannewa**/St. Ewe near **St. Austell**/Sen Ostell. **Lannewa**/St. Ewe was the place where a girl told of two older women speaking *'English and Kernowok'* in 1596.

Ewdi m.

The Cornwall Subsidies record this name as *Ewdy Bocher* of **Kammbronn**/Camborne in 1545. See also **Udi**.

Ewik f.

This name in modern **Kernewek** means 'doe, hind'.

Ewryn m.

In the Cornwall Military Survey of 1522, there is an *Ewryn Fyttoke* recorded as living in the parish of **Lannudhno**/St Erth and armed with bow and 12 arrows. There was also an *Ewryn Briand* of **Kammbronn**/Camborne.

Ewstek m.

This name is found in the Cornish place-name **Porthewstek**/Porthoustock on the Lizard.

Eyger f.

She was the wife of **Gorloes** and mother of **Arthur**. This is also an equivalent to the Welsh Eigr.

Eythin f.

This name in **Kernewek** means 'gorse'.

Felan m.

This name is from OB and found in the place-name Bofindle.

Felek m.

From Latin Felicitas and found in Cornish form in the place-name Bephillick.

Fenten f.

This name in **Kernewek** means 'spring, fountain' and is found in place-names right across the country.

Fiega f.

This feminine form of **Fiek** is recorded in very early documents. This name has three syllables i.e. Fi-EG-a. See **Fiek**

Fiek m.

A saint's name recorded at the village of **Sen Fiek**/Feock that lies at the head of the Carrick Roads. There is a Breton name, Fieg, a variant of Fiakr, which may be a cognate to **Fiek**. This name has two syllables and is pronounced FI-ek.

Fili m.

The village of **Eglosros**/Philleigh is found on the bank of the River Fal.

Fimbarrus m.

A Latin version of St. Finbarr, bishop of Cork. The Cornish claim that he crossed the Celtic Sea on horseback and is buried at **Fowydh**/Fowey.

Finna f.

This name means 'finer' and is taken from **Gerlyver Meur**.

Fleghik m.

In **Kernewek** means 'little child'. The <gh> is pronounced as a heavy [h].

Fowenn f.

Another name from **Kernewek** meaning 'beech tree'.

Fowi f.

This is the Cornish river–name meaning 'river of beech trees'. The town in **Kernewek** is called **Fowydh** meaning beech trees.

Friek m.

Found in all three Brythonnic languages, OB, OC and OW, it is found in the early tenth century Bodmin Manumissions. **Friek** is found in the place-name Trefreock and was a nick name meaning 'big nose'.

Fylip m.

A Cornish spelling of Welsh Phylip and equivalent of English Philip. See also **Fylipa**.

Fylipa f.

A feminine form of the above name and so equivalent to English Philippa.

Gall m.

This name is from OW and found in the place-name Badgall.

Garki m.

This personal name from OW is found in the place-name Chygarkye, combined with **chi** 'house'.

Gari m.

This is simply a Cornish respelling of the English name Gary. **Gari an Gov** sings in **Kernewek** with the rock band **Mammvro**. As he practices Cornish wrestling and karate I'm not going to argue with him over how he spells his name!

Garmon m.

This name is found in the place-name Tregwarmond and may be found in Trewarmett.

Garth m.

An equivalent of English Gareth or Welsh Garth.

Gavran m.

This name is found in the Cornish place-name of Portgaverne from **porth** 'cove, harbour' + **Gavran**.

Gawen m.

Equivalent of English Gavin and Welsh Gawain. He was a hero of the Arthurian legends. **Gawen** has been increasingly used amongst Cornish speakers in the last twenty years. See also **Gawena**.

Gawena f.

A feminine form of the above name.

Gelvinek m.

In **Kernewek** this has the meaning of 'curlew'. It is also the bardic name of Cornish songwriter and expert on Late Cornish, **Richard Gendall**.

Gennys m.

This saint is honoured at St. Gennys in the north of the country.

Genver m. or f.

This would make a good name for a baby born in the month of January.

Gerens m.

There are a number of legends about Geraint in Wales, Scotland and of course Cornwall. Gerrans Bay lies on the south coast of Cornwall. The name may also be found in the place-name Resurrance, combined with **rys** meaning 'ford'. The Cornwall Subsidies of 1543 record a *Gerens Vyn* of **Lannsiek**/St. Just in Roseland and a *Gerance Trenerthe* of **Lanngostentin**/Constantine.

Gerannus m.

In the Military Survey of 1522 there is a *Gerannus Bodregy* also recorded as living in the parish of St Gluvyas. This same man is also recorded as *Gerendus Bodregy*. This may be a latinization of **Gerens**. See also **Gerens**.

Germogh m.

He is remembered at the village of **Sen Germogh**/Germoe near **Marghasyow**/Marazion, in West Cornwall.

Gildas m.

He was a 6th century author who wrote *De excidio et conquestu Britanniae* telling us of the Angle, Saxon and Jutish invasions of Celtic Britain. **Gildas** came from the British Kingdom of Strathclyde and travelled through Cornwall, finally dying in Brittany.

Glasan m.

This name is from OW and found in the place-name Chylason. See **Glasena**.

Glasana f.

A feminine form of the above name.

Glander f.

A new name for girls which means 'purity'.

Glanna f.

This name is from **Kernewek** and means 'purer'.

Glanmer m.

A Cornish version of the Welsh name Glanmor and means 'great and pure'.

Glevyas m.

He is the patron of **Sen Gluvyas**/St. Gluvias near **Aberfal**/Falmouth and means 'clear, bright'. **Glevyas** has his feast day on May the 3rd.

Glynn m.

This name from **Kernewek** that means 'large valley,' **nans** being the more common word for valley. It is also an equivalent for Welsh Glyn or Glynn. See also **Glynna**.

Glynna f.

A Cornish feminine form of the above name.

Goedhyan m.

He has his church at **Sen Goedhyan**/Gwithian near **Heyl**/Hayle. His oratory was buried by the shifting sands of the Red River. There was also a 6th century pagan chief from North Cornwall who had the same name. **Goedhyan** the saint was converted by St. Samson.

Golow m.

This name in **Kernewek** means 'bright, light, brilliant'.

Golowa f.

A new name and the feminine form of **Golow**.

Golowan m.

Another name from Brittany being found in OB and in the Cornish place-name Trewolland, (combined with **tre** 'farm, settlement, home').

Golvan m.

This name in **Kernewek** means 'sparrow'. **Golvan** is the bardic name of **Nicholas Williams** the Celtic Studies expert in Ireland.

Gonnetta f.

This was a common name for girls in 14th century Cornwall.

Gorabo m.

This name is found in the Cornish place-name Treboe; **tre** 'farm, settlement' + **Gorabo**.

Goran m.

This saint was a hermit who gave shelter to **Petrek** and giving his name to a well at **Bosvenegh**/Bodmin and to **Lannworan**/Gorran Churchtown and **Porthyust**/Gorran Haven in Mid Cornwall. The Cornwall Subsidies record this name as *Goran Thomas* of **Elerghi**/Veryan in 1543.

Gordhavo m.

This name is found in the Cornish place-name Tredavoe which is derived from **tre** 'farm, settlement' + **Gordhavo**.

Gordhylik m.

This name is from OC and OW and means 'very beloved'. **Gordhylik** is also found in the place-name Trethillick.

Gorega f.

A feminine form of the name below.

Gorek m.

Another ancient Celtic name this time taken from the place-name Rosewarrick. See also **Gorega**.

Goreu m.

In the Arthurian triad of *The Three Very Famous Prisoners of the Island of Britain* he was properly *Goreu vab Custennin*, cousin of **Arthur,** who released him from prison.

Gorgan m.

This name is from OB and found in the place-name Bodrugan.

Gorgans m.

From OC, found in the early tenth century Bodmin Manumissions and may mean 'very white'. **Gorgans** is found in the place-name Treworgans.

Gorgen m.

This name is derived from British *vor-genos* and came to Cornwall via OB. **Gorgen** has the meaning of 'super born'.

Gorgenyw m.

OW gave rise to this name and is found in the place-name Tregenna in Lamorrab.

Gorgi m.

This funny but popular name is from OC and found in many place-names throughout Cornwall. The name literally means 'super dog'. See **Raglavar**/Introduction.

Gorgu m.

The Cornwall Subsidies of 1543 records a *Gorgu Lynam* of **Lanndogho**/St. Kew.

Gorgwynn m.

This name is from OW and found in the place-name Chygwidden in Lelant. At first glance the place-name appears to be derived from **chi** 'house' + **gwynn** 'white' but in 1335, a time when **Kernewek** was spoken right across Cornwall, the name was written *Chigurgwyn*. The name seems to mean 'very white, fair or holy'.

Gorhaval m.

This name is from OW and found in the place-name Wrasford.

Gorhi m.

This name is found in the Cornish place-name which is derived from **tre** 'farm, settlement' + **Gorhi**.

Gorhyder m.

From the ancient British *vor-setros* and means 'very bold'. **Gorhyder** then continued into OC and OW and is found in the early tenth century Bodmin Manumissions. It is found in the place-name Treworder in **Ruan Vyghan**/Ruan Minor.

Gorlas m.

This name is from OB and OW and found in the place-name Treworlas. **Gorlas** may mean 'very pure, holy'.

Gorman m.

This name is found in the Cornish place-name Trewarmett which is derived from **tre** 'farm, settlement' + **Gorman**.

Gormel m.

A good strong name taken from **Kernewek** which means 'praise'.

Gormela f.

This name is the feminine form of **Gormel** and in **Kernewek** also means 'praise'.

Gorneves m.

This name is from OW and found in the place-name Trewarnevas.

Goronan m.

This name is found in the place-name Trewornan and may mean 'super one'.

Gorthalan m.

Another name from the place-names of Cornwall and may be found in Burthallan.

Gortheren f.

This would be a great name for a girl born in the month of July.

Gorthogi m.

This name is from OW and may be found in the place-name Borthog.

Gorvil m.

This name is from OW and found in the place-name Roscorwell.

Gorvo m.

From OB and found in the place-name Treverva, **tre** 'settlement, farm' + **Gorvo**. **Treverva Male Voice Choir** is one of Cornwall's great choirs.

Gorvoy m.

This name is found in the Cornish place-name Rejerrah which is derived from **rys** 'ford' + **Gorvoy**.

Gorvyw m.

This name is from OW and found in the place-name Trevorrow. This has given rise to the family-name, Trevorrow. A certain Tommy Trevorrow was a miner who would not leave a crust for Bucca (a bad underground spirit) and was cursed for being miserly;

> "Tommy Trevorrow, Tommy Trevorrow,
> Bad luck on 'ee tomorrow!"

Gorwal m.

Also found in OB and may be found in the place-name Treword.

Gorwalls m.

This name is found in the place-name Trewolvas.

Gorwydh m.

This name is from OW and found in the place-name Trewarrow.

Goryen m.

From the ancient British *vor-genos* 'well-born'. **Goryen** is also found in OB as *Uuorien* and found in the Cornish place-name Treworyan.

Gossenek f.

In **Kernewek** means 'rusty'. This would be a great name for a red haired baby!

Gov m.

In modern Kernewek this means 'smith'. **Mighal Yosep** the leader of the Cornish in the 1497 war with the English was known as **An Gov** 'the smith'. The spelling *An Gof* as seen on various walls is archaic and a Welshism.

Govannown m

This is the Cornish version of the Welsh name Gofannon. **Govannown** was the Celtic god of smiths, like the god Jupiter.

Goven m.

This name is from OW and found in the place-name Becovan.

Govenek m.

Taken from **Gerlyver Meur** this name means 'hope'.

Growan m.

Taken from **Kernewek** this strong name means 'granite'.

Grug f.

This is the Cornish version of the English name Heather.

Grugwynn m.

A Cornish version of the Welsh name Grugwyn meaning 'white, fair heather'.

Grugwynna f.

This is the feminine version of the Welsh Grugwyn.

Gryffyn m.

This Celtic name is found as a landowner in the Domesday Book for Cornwall and in OW and also OC in the early tenth century Bodmin Manumissions.

Gwalader m.

This name is from OB and OW and means 'leader'. **Gwalader** is also found in the place-name Trewalder.

Gwallek m.

This name is from OW and found in Cornwall in the place-name Trewollack.

Gwarghan m.

Again from OW and found in this country in the place-name Boswarthan.

Gwarier m.

This means 'actor, player' in **Kernewek** and has been used as a bardic name.

Gwariores f.

From **Gerlyver Meur** this is a feminine form of **Gwarier** and so means 'actress, female player'.

Gwas m.

This name may be found in the place-name Boswas and had the meaning of 'chap, bloke, fellow' but now has the meaning of 'servant'.

Gwasso m.

A peculiarly Cornish name being from OC and found in the place-name Trewassa.

Gwasyn m.

In the Arthurian triad of *Kulhogh and Olwen* he could stamp a mountain flat.

Gwavas m.

Gwav is **Kernewek** for winter and **bos** means 'dwelling'. **Gwavas** is a compound meaning 'winter dwelling' and reveals that the Cornish used to practice transhumance. **Gwavas** is also a bardic name and a family-name. **William Gwavas** was an 18th century Cornish language scholar. See also **Gwavasa**.

Gwavasa f.

A feminine form of the above name.

Gwaytyans f.

In **Kernewek** this has the meaning of 'hope' and has been used as a bardic name as well.

Gwedhenek m.

Found in **Lannwedhenek** (**lann** 'holy enclosure' + **Gwedhenek**) the Cornish form of Padstow. A Breton version of this name survives today as the Breton family-name Guezennec. **Lannwedhenek** became Padstow on the arrival of St. Petrok and the name became corrupted to Lodenek – the name of a Cornish publishing house and bungalow estate in Padstow town.

Gwegen m.

This name is from OB and may be found in the place-name Lambriggan near **Porthpyran**/Perranporth.

Gwelenn f.

Gerlyver Meur provides this magical name and in modern **Kernewek** means 'wand' or 'mast'.

Gweles m.

This peculiarly Cornish name being from OC may be found in the place-name Trewillis. In **Kernewek** the verb to see is **gweles** and there may be a link with the personal name.

Gweloegan m.

From OW and may be found in the East Cornwall place-name Trelawne in Pelynt.

Gwelvel f.

She has her church at **Lannystli**/Gulval near **Pennsans**/Penzance.

Gwenbros m.

This name may be found in the place-name Trobus.

Gwendern m.

Found in the early tenth century Bodmin Manumissions and means 'white, splendid lord', the last element being British *tegerno* 'lord'.

Gwendron m.

Egloswendron/Wendron is near **Hellys**/Helston. There have been female forms of this name – see **Gwendrona**.

Gwendrona f.

The church to this saint is found at **Egloswendron**/Wendron, near **Hellys**/Helston. There have been male forms of this name. See also **Gwendron**.

Gwenek m.

This name is found in the Cornish place-name Lewannick which is derived from **lann** 'enclosure' + **Gwenek**.

Gwenepa f.

She was one of the 24 children of King Brychan of Wales. This remarkable family went on to found churches all over the Celtic world. Gwennap near **Rysrudh**/Redruth is **Lannwenep** in **Kernewek** and was known in English as *St. Weneppa* in 1281. Her name also survives as Gwennap Pit, the site where Methodists hold their great gatherings.

Gwener f.

This name from **Gerlyver Meur** means 'Venus, the planet'. **Dy'Gwener** means Friday. This name is already in use for girls born on a Friday.

Gwengor m.

Another very Cornish name being from OC and found in the place-name Boswinger.

Gwenheden f.

She was another one of the 24 children of King Brychan of Wales. This great family went on to found churches all over the Celtic world including the one at St. Enodoc which is dedicated to **Gwenheden.**

Gwenki f.

She was one of the lesser known saints of the 24 children of King Brychan. **Gwenki** is recorded as *Wencu* and is honoured at **Lanndogho**/St. Kew.

Gwenna f.

Yet another of the 24 children of Brychan and is remembered at the village of **Sen Gwenna**/St. Wenn, near Bodmin. **Gwenna** has her feast day on October the 18th. **Nonna's** sister was also named **Gwenna**. Forms with the initial <g> but with the final <a> are to be avoided. See **Gwynna.**

Gwennega f.

A feminine form of the name below.

Gwennek m.

This name is from OW and found in the West Cornwall place-name Boswednack. See also **Gwennega**.

Gwennel f.

This name in **Kernewek** means 'swallow'. **Gwennel** is the bardic name of **Sue Smith** who founded **Dalleth** – the Cornish language organisation for children.

Gwensens f.

She was one of the 24 children of King Brychan of Wales. This family then went on to found churches all over the Celtic world. **Gwensens** is remembered at Lezant. However the place-name may be derived from **lann** 'enclosure' + **sans** 'holy'.

Gwenton m.

This poetic name in **Kernewek** meaning 'spring season'.

Gwentena f.

This a feminized form of **Gwenton**.

Gweri m.

A name is from OB and found in the place-names Calvorry and Trewerry.

Gwethen m.

This name is from OW and found in the place-name Treweatha.

Gweryr m.

The patron of the church at **Sen Niet**/St. Neot. See **Niet**.

Gwethgen m.

This name is from OB and found in the place-name Trewithian.

Gwethek m.

Another name, probably from a pioneer farmer from the sisterland being found in OB and found in the place-name Trevithick at **Sen Kolomm**/St. Columb.

Gwethis m.

From both OC and OW and found in the place-name Carwither.

Gwethor m.

This name is from OB and found in the place-name Trewetha.

Gwethyen m.

A mysterious name of Celtic origin and found in the place-name Lanwithan. See also **Kogwethyen**.

Gwiryon f.

This name in **Kernewek** means 'just, true, righteous'.

Gwlesik m.

Derived from OB and could have the meaning 'nation' being based on **gwlas** 'nation, country' as in **Penn an Wlas**/Lands End.

Gwoeswal m.

This name is from OB and OW and found in the place-names Tregoodwell and Truthall.

Gwydhek m.

This name is from OW and found in the place-name Bowithick.

Gwydhel m.

Found in all three Brythonic languages, i.e. in OB, OC and OW as Guital. **Gwydhel** is also found combined with **bos** 'dwelling' in the place-name Boswiddle. See **Gwydhela**.

Gwydhela f.

A feminine form of the above name.

Gwydhelan m.

Another ancient name from OW and may be found in Cornwall in the place-name Trewidland. However the second element in the place-name may be **gwydhlann** 'plantation'.

Gwydhenn f.

This rather hippy name in **Kernewek** means 'tree'.

Gwydhgi m.

According to Gover this name is from OW and found in the place-name Trewirgie.

Gwydhnow m.

This name is from OW and found in the place-name Trewithnow.

Gwydhvos f.

This is the collective name in **Kernewek** for 'honeysuckle'.

Gwydhvosenn f.

In **Kernewek** this name has the meaning of 'a honeysuckle plant'. **Gwydhvosenn** is the bardic name of **Jenefer Lowe**, Cornish speaker and leading member of **Ros Keltek**.

Gwyger m.

Another name from OW and found in the place-name Trewigger.

Gwyllek m.

He was beheaded by his brother, **Melyn**, and picked up his own head and carried it to the site of **Sen Gwyllow**/St. Willow. There is another form of his name. See **Gwyllow**.

Gwyllow m.

There is another form of his name. See **Gwyllek**.

Gwynn m.

Another name of a pioneer farmer and found in the place-name Boswedden and means 'fair, white'.

Gwynna f.

Also the equivalent to Breton Gwenn and French Blanche. Forms without the final –a are to be avoided as **gwenn** is **Kernewek** for 'anus'.

Gwynnan m.

This name is from OB and OW and found in the place-name West Cornwall place-name Boswednan. Again at first glance, this looks like **bos** 'dwelling' with a Late Cornish form of **gwynn** 'white, fair'. However the name was written as *Boswynnan* in 1289, 1314 and 1333. Pre-occlusion occurred centuries later showing that the place-name is derived from the personal name; **Gwynnan**.

Gwynnda f.

This is the Cornish version of the Welsh name Gwenda and means 'white, fair and good'.

Gwynndal m.

A Cornish equivalent for the Breton Gwenndal and means 'white, fair brow'. See also **Talwynn**.

Gwynnder f.

This name from **Gerlyver Meur** and in **Kernewek** means 'holiness, saintliness'.

Gwynnek m.

Remembered at **Sen Gwynnow**/St. Winnow, near **Fowydh**/Fowey and has his feast day on the 6th of November. A possible meaning of this name is 'saintly'. The Breton form of this name is Gwenneg. **Gwynnek** is from OB and OW and found in the place-name Trewinnick. See also **Gwynnow**.

Gwynneres m.

This very Cornish name is from OC and may be found in the place-name Trenarret.

Gwynnfrosa f.

This is the Cornish version of the Welsh name Gwenffrwd and has the meaning 'white stream'.

Gwynngala f.

In **Kernewek** this has the literal meaning of 'white straw' and is the word for September. It has already been used for a girl's name and so that practice is followed here.

Gwynnhel m.

This name is a Cornish equivalent for the Breton Gwenaël and means 'white and generous'. See also **Gwynnhelek**.

Gwynnhelek m.

A name is derived from British *uindos *saglos-akos*. **Gwynnhelek** is found in OB and meaning 'white and abounding in generousity'. It is found in the place-name Trenhellick. Gwynhellic Films of **Pennsans**/Penzance have adopted a Welsh version of this name. See also **Gwynnhel**.

Gwynniver f.

A earlier form of **Jenefer** based on Welsh Gwenifer. She was, of course, the wife of **Arthur**.

Gwynnliwa f.

Cornish version of the Welsh name Gwenlliw and means 'white or fair colour'.

Gwynnow m.

He is remembered at **Sen Gwynnow**/St. Winnow. **Gwynnow's** feast day is 6th November. The personal name is from OB and OW and found in the place-name Trewinnow in **Bre Gledh**/North Hill. See also **Gwynnek**.

Gwynnvel m.

Cornish equivalent for the Breton Gwenvael and means 'white, fair prince'.

Gwynnvrewi f..

Equivalent of English Winifred or Welsh Gwenfrewi.

Gwynnvronn f

This is the Cornish version of the Welsh name Gwenfron and means 'fair, white breast'.

Gwynnvys m.

Gerlyver Meur is the source for this name and in Kernewek means 'bliss'.

Gwynnwalow m.

He is patron saint of **Lanndewynnek**/Landewednack on the Lizard Peninsula and Lanndevenneg (Breton name)/Landévennec (French name). His mother was a Breton called Alba Trimammis, 'white three-breasts', who had triplets and so grew a third breast. **Gwynnwalow** also restored his sister's eye which had been pecked out and swallowed by a goose! He is also patron of **Tewynnek**/Towednack near **Porthia**/St. Ives and **Treven**/Tremaine, near **Lannstefan**/Launceston. The feast day of this great Celtic saint is March the 3rd.

Gwynnyer m.

His church is situated at Sen **Gwynnyer**/Gwinear, near **Heyl**/Hayle and he, with his 777 Irish companions, was killed by the pagan Cornish king **Tewder**.

Gwynnyow m.

This name may be found in the place-name Trenio.

Gwynnys m.

The village of **Sen Gwynnys**/St. Gennys is situated in the north-east of the country and his feast day is 2nd May.

Gwystyl m.

This name is from OW and found in the place-names Trusell in Tremaine.

Gwythenek m.

A name of another pioneer farmer from Brittany and found in the West Cornwall place-name of Carwythenack.

Gwyther m.

Equivalent of Welsh Gwythyr and English Victor. Gwyther comes from OB and OW and found in the place-name Hendraweather (**hendra** 'home farm + **Gwyther**).

Gwytherin m.

This name is from OW and found in the place-name Trewethern.

Gynnek m.

In the Cornwall Subsidies for 1545 a *Gynnock Power* is recorded as living in **Sen Hyleri**/St. Hilary.

Harri m.

A pet form of Henry and in Cornish spelling, Welsh Harri.

Hav m.

This name is from **Kernewek** and means 'summer'. The name is also found in Wales as Haf but is a girls' name.

Havgan f.

Cornish version of the Welsh name Hafgan and means 'summer song'.

Hebaska f.

From **Gerlyver Meur** this name in **Kernewek** means 'solace'.

Hebes m.

This name is from OB and found in the place-name Tresibbet on Bodmin Moor. However the place-name may contain **sybwydh** 'fir trees'.

Hedra f.

A girl born in October could use this name. Bice has listed this as feminine and that practice is followed here.

Hegar f.

In **Kernewek** this name has the meaning of 'kindly'. **Hegar** is not to be confused with the word **hager** 'ugly' or the cartoon character Hagar the Horrible!

Hegoel m.

This name from **Gerlyver Meur** in **Kernewek** means 'trustful'.

Hegoela f.

The feminine form of **Hegoel** and also means 'trustful'.

Helek m.

This boys' name is from OB and may be found in the place-name Bottallick. However the place-name may be derived from **bos** 'dwelling' + **talek** 'sloping'.

Helghyer m.

This strong sounding name in **Kernewek** means 'hunter'.

Helghyores f.

From **Gerlyver Meur** this name means 'huntress'.

Heligenn f.

In modern **Kernewek** means 'willow tree'. Remember the stress falls on the middle syllable; Hel-I-genn and the <i> is pronounced like <ee> in English 'queen'. The Cornish academic and writer, **Myrna Combellack**, took this as her bardic name.

Henben m.

This name is from OW and found in the place-name Trehemborne.

Henna m.

This is a Cornish pet form of Henry.

Hepkenyn m.

This mysterious name is found in the place-name Trekenning, spelt *Trehepkenyn* in 1294.

Hergi m.

The name is from OW and found in the place-name Lanhargy.

Hernow m.

This name is found in the Cornish place-name Lanherne, *Lanherno* 1257 which is derived from **lann** 'enclosure' + **Hernow**.

Heyl m.

He was one of the lesser known children of King Brychan of Wales. His name may occur at **Eglosheyl**/Egloshayle but this is more likely to be **eglos** 'church' + **heyl** 'estuary'.

Hilin m.

This name is from OW and found in the place-name Nanhellan. See also **Hilina**.

Hilina f.

A feminine form of the above name.

Hoghan m.

This name is again from Wales but found in the Cornish place-name Bossoughan.

Hokki m.

In the Cornwall Military Survey of 1522 there is a *Hokky Carvynek* recorded as living in the parish of **Sen Ke**/Kea.

Hornek m.

This name is from OW and may be found in the place-name Castle-Horneck. The place may include **hornek** 'iron bearing (ground)'.

Hornwallon m.

Found in the early tenth century Bodmin Manumissions and derived from the British *isarnouallanos* which is derived from a root meaning 'iron'.

Hoskyn m.

Although now only used as a family-name **Hoskyn** is recorded as a Christian name. In the Cornwall Military Survey of 1522 there is a *Hoskin Engove* of **Lanngostentin**/Constanine and a *Hoskyn Payne* of **Pyranudhno**/Perranuthnoe.

Howel m.

This was the name of the Cornish king who witnessed the surrender of the Welsh princes to Athelstan (died 940) at Exeter. **Howel** means 'eminent'. The MP for **Bosvenegh**/Bodmin in 1327 was *Howel de Cruglas*. The family-name is derived from **krug** 'barrow, mound' + **glas** 'green'.

Howlyek f.

Another modern **Kernewek** name meaning 'sunny'. **Howlek** in **Kernewek** means 'solar'.

Huberth m.

This is the Cornish equivalent to Breton Huberzh and French Hubert.

Humfra m.

The Cornwall Subsidies of 1543 records *Humffra Harlyn* and *Humffra Richard* both of **Eglosvrega**/Breage. **Humfra** with its <a> for <y> appears to be a Cornish form of Humphrey.

Hunros f.

Gerlyver Meur gives us this delightful name which means 'dream'.

Hunyes m.

This name is found in the Cornish place-name Menheniot which is derived from **ma** 'plain, plateau' + **Hunyes**.

Hwegynn f.

This name in **Kernewek** means 'little sweet thing' and is derived from **hweg** 'sweet'.

Hwekka f.

In **Kernewek** means 'sweeter' and is derived from **hweg** meaning 'sweet'.

Hwevrer m.

This name means February and is masculine because it is found in the place-name **Pollhwevrer**/Polwheveral near **Aberfal**/Falmouth.

Hydrek m.

A saint who gave his name to **Lannhydrek**/Lanhydroc, near **Bosvenegh**/Bodmin. His feast day is 5th of May. **Hydrek**, also found in OW, is based on a root meaning 'bold'.

Hykk m.

This is an abbreviated form of **Hykka**. In the Cornwall Military Survey of 1522 there is a *Hyck Richard* recorded as living in the parish of Stratton and a *Hyc' Lethan* of **Lannyust**/St. Just in Penwith. See also **Hykka**.

Hykka m.

This is a Cornish pet form and so equivalent of Richard. In the Cornwall Military Survey of 1522 there is a *Hycka Lethon* recorded as living in the parish of **Lannyust**/St Just in Penwith. William Gwavas, a Cornish Scholar of the 18th century records this name as *Hecca*. Here it is respelled in modern **Kernewek**. See also **Hykk**.

Hyldren m.

He was a bishop and became confused with the patron saint of **Lannsalwys**/Lansallos, near Looe. See **Ilderna**.

Hynek m.

Another pioneer farmer with a Breton name and found in the Cornish place-name Polinnick, near **Pederwynn Dheghow**/South Petherwin.

Hyvyo m.

According to Gover this name is from OW and found in the place-name Trevio.

Ia f.

She floated to Cornwall on a leaf and **Dinan**, a local chieftain, built her church at **Porthia**/St. Ives. Her feast day is on the 3rd February. See **Dinan**.

Igerna f.

She was the wife of **Gorloes** a Cornish duke and supposedly mother of **Arthur**. See also **Eyger**.

Ilderna f.

She is the patron saint of **Lannsalwys**/Lansallos, near **Logh**/Looe. In the 15th century she was confused with a bishop named **Hyldren**. See **Hyldren**.

Illogan m.

Nothing is known of this mysterious saint whose name survives in the English name of **Egloshal**/Illogan. The Cornish form derives from **eglos** 'church' + **hal** 'moorland'.

Ilow m.

This romantic name in **Kernewek** means 'music'.

Ilowa f.

This very poetic name from **Gerlyver Meur** also means 'music'.

Isi m.

He gave his name to the English name of **Egloskrug**/St. Issey, near **Ponsrys**/Wadebridge (the Cornish name is derived from **eglos** 'church' + **krug** 'burial mound') and also to Mevagissey, which derives from S. Meva + **hag** 'and' S. Isi. He was one of the 24 children of King Brychan of Wales.

Iswal m.

Gover states this name is from OW and found in the place-name Trudgewell.

Iv m.

A Cornish bishop who gave his name to **Sen Iv**/St. Ive, near **Kelliwik**/Callington and St. Ives in Cambridgeshire. His feast day is April 24th. **Sen Iv**/St. Ive has hosted a Cornish language Carol Service every year since 1978.

Iwerdhon f.

This name in **Kernewek** means 'Ireland' and would be a great name for someone of Irish descent.

Jago m.

Equivalent of English James and Welsh Iago. **Bredereth Sen Jago** is the Catholic group who honour St. James of Compestella. See also **Yago**.

Jakka m.

This is a Cornish equivalent of English Jack. In the Cornwall Military Survey there is a *Jacka Thomas* of **Sen Gwynnyer**/Gwinear and a *Jacka Rodda* of **Egloskrowenna**/Crowan.

Jakys m.

In the Cornwall Subsidies for 1545 a *Jakys Breton, alien* is recorded as living in **Egloshal**/Illogan. This looks like a Cornish version of the modern Breton name Jakez, itself a version of French Jacques.

Jamma m.

This was an early Cornish pet form of James.

Jamys m.

Equivalent of English James. In the Cornwall Military Survey of 1522 there is a *Jamys Thomas* recorded as living in the parish of **Lanngostentin**/Constantine.

Jana f.

This name is an alternative form of **Jenna**.

Jeffer m.

The Cornwall Subsidies record this name as *Jeffer Halse* **Logsulyen**/Luxulyan in 1543. This is an earlier pet form of Geoffrey. See also **Jeffra**.

Jeffra m.

Cornish pet form of Geoffrey. See also **Jeffer**.

Jellyan m.

In the Cornwall Subsidies for 1545 a *Jellyan, servant and alien* is recorded as living in **Eglosvadern**/Madron.

Jellyn m.

The Cornwall Subsidies record this name as *Jellyn Badcock* of **Fowydh**/Fowey and as *Gelyan Bretton* of Keynwynn/Kenwyn in 1543. The second person is recorded as an 'alien' and so perhaps **Jellyn** was brought over from our sister country of Brittany. See **Jellyan**.

Jenefer f.

Equivalent of Welsh Gwenhwyfar and Gwenifer.

Jenkyn m.

Although a family name, it is used as a Christian name. In the Cornwall Military Survey of 1522 there is a *Jenkin Killyvregh* recorded as living in the parish of **Egloshal**/Illogan.

Jenna f.

The Cornish version of English Jane. In Cornish dialect a 'jenna' is a doll. **Jenna** is one of the characters featured in the weekly **Kernewek** Column in the Western Morning News. See also **Jana**.

Jenyn m.

In the Cornwall Military Survey there is a *Janyn Pascowe* of **Egloskuri**/Cury. Also in the Cornwall Subsidies of 1525 there is a *Gensyn Dawe* of **Nanseglos**/Lanteglos by Camelford.

Jermen m.

This is the Cornish version of Breton Jermen and French Germain. Also in the Cornwall Subsidies of 1545 there is a *Jerman Harris* of **Tewynnek**/Towednack. The name was found ouside the country but remained popular in Cornwall due to St. Germanus being patron of **Lannaled**/St. Germans and **Penn an Hordh**/Rame.

Jilberth m.

Cornish version of Breton Jilberzh and French Jilberth.

Jori m.

Equivalent of English George and Welsh Siôr. See also **Joria**. **Jori Ansell** is a former **Bardh Meur**/Grand Bard and chair of the European Lesser Used Language Bureau (Cornish Branch).

Joria f.

A feminine form of Jori and so an equivalent to English Georgina. See **Jori**.

Jorwerth m.

Equivalent of English Edward, Ed and Eddy and also Welsh Iorwerth. See also **Yorwerth**.

Josep m.

Equivalent of English Joseph, Jo and Joey as well as Welsh Iago. The Cornwall Subsidies record this as a Christian name; *John Josepp* of **Sen Niwlin**/Newlyn East in 1543.

Josepa f.

A Cornish equivalent of Breton Josefa and French Joséphine. **Nyns yw haneth Josepa** – as Napolian would have said if he had been a Cornish speaker.

Jowann m.

This is an equivalent of English John, Welsh Ieuan and Breton Yann. The name is also found in the place-names Troan and Treyone. **Jowann Richards** is the prolific Cornish language writer. See also **Yowann**.

Jowannet f.

Feminine version of **Jowann** and equivalent of English Janet. See also **Yowannet**.

Jowav m.

According to Gover this name is from OW and found in the place-name Bodieve. However Padel believes that the name is derived from **bos** 'dwelling' + **yuv** 'lord'. See **Yowav**.

Jowl m.

In **Kernewek** means 'devil' – a jokey, rather than a serious name for a pet!

Jowles f.

This in **Kernewek** means 'she devil' and would be good for a badly behaved female pet.

Jowlik m.

Using the **–ik** suffix this name in **Kernewek** means 'little devil' – a great name for a mischievous puppy or kitten.

Juliot f.

She is listed as one of the 24 children of King Brychan of Wales. Her name is remembered at **Nanseglos**/Lanteglos. Her feast day is 16th June.

Judans m.

Another OB name found in the Cornish place-name Trythance. See also **Yudans**.

Judek m.

According to Gover this name is from OB and found in the place-name Trethick. See also **Yudek**.

Judel m.

This name is from OB and found in the place-names Bodithiel, Trethill and Truthall. See also **Yudel**.

Judreth m.

Another strange name from OB and found in the place-name Trehudreth. See also **Yudreth**.

Judno m.

From both OB and OW and found in the place-name Trudnoe. See also **Yudno**.

Jungi m.

Another OB name found in the place-name Lesingey. See also **Yungi**.

Junhern m.

According to Gover this name may be found in the place-name Rejame. See also **Yunhern**.

Junwal m.

This name is from OB and found in the place-name Laninwell. See also **Yunwal**.

Junwyth m.

This name is found in the place-name Trenwith. At first glance this appears to be **tre** 'farm, settlement' + **an** 'the' + **gwydh** 'trees' but the name was spelt *Treyunwith* in 1391 and *Treunwith* in 1508 which reveals the personal name of **Junwyth** or **Yunwyth**. See also **Yunwyth**.

Just m.

His name is remembered at **Lannyust**/St. Just in Penwith and **Lannsiek**/St. Just in Roseland. If the Cornish names are used there is no need for the 'in Penwith' and 'in Roseland'. See also **Yust**.

Juswal m.

This name is from OB and OW and found combined with **nans** 'valley' in the place-name Nansidwell. See also **Yuswal**.

Jylli m.

This is a Cornish equivalent of Breton Jili, French Gilles and English Giles.

Kabel m.

This was the name of **Arthur's** hound according to the ancient *Book of Nennius*. See also **Kabela**.

Kabela f.

A feminine form of the above name.

Kadek m.

This is an older form of **Kasek**. See **Kasek** and **Kesega**.

Kader m.

This name in **Kernewek** means 'warrior, handsome'. **Kader** was a Cornish Earl in the time of **Arthur**. **Chris James** of **Spit**, winners of the 1999 Pan-Keltek Song Contest, uses this name as a nom de plume.

Kadores f.

A name from **Gerlyver Meur** and with the meaning 'she warrior'. See also **Kader**.

Kadyles m.

This name is found in the Cornish place-name of Tregadillett < **tre** 'farm, settlement' + **Kadyles**.

Kaja f.

A name in **Kernewek** that means 'daisy'.

Kantalon m.

Nothing is known of this Celtic name except that according to Gover it is found in the place-name Tregantallon.

Kara f.

Using the Cornish verb 'to love' this is the Cornish version of the Welsh name Cari 'to love'.

Karansek m.

He is venerated at **Lanngorrow**/Crantock, near **Tewynn Bleustra**/Newquay. **Arthur** called upon this Welsh saint to take on a dragon. **Karansek** captured the beast, stopped **Arthur's** soldier from killing it and let it go on the promise that it behaved itself.

Karasek m.

This name is from OB and OW and found in the place-names Tregardock and Tregassick. **Karasek** has the meaning 'amiable'. This was the name of a legendary Duke of Cornwall and chieften.

Karer m.

This name in **Kernewek** means 'lover, friend'.

Kares f.

This name in **Kernewek** means 'a female lover or friend'.

Karol f.

This is the common English name Carol, simply respelled in **Kernewek**.

Karrek f.

Again from **Gerlyver Meur** this strong sounding name in **Kernewek** means 'rock'.

Karwynn m.

Cornish version of the Welsh feminine name Carwen and has the meaning 'fair love'. See **Karwynna**.

Karwynna f.

Feminine Cornish version of the Welsh name Carwen and also means 'fair love'. See **Karwynn**.

Kasan m.

Another name also found in Welsh but also found in the Cornish place-name of Roscadden.

Kasega f.

A feminine form of the name below.

Kasek m.

This name is found in OW and in the Cornish place-name Boscadjack. **Kasek** is also a Cornish saint who has a holy well and chapel at **Arlynn**/Harlyn Bay on the north Cornish coast. He floated on a cloud to Benevento, Italy, where he became bishop and met a martyr's death while celebrating Mass. **Kasek** was one of the three knights who kept the Holy Grail. See also **Kasega**.

Kasnow m.

This heroic name is from OC and OW and also found in the place-name Boscathnoe. **Kasnow** means 'battle famous'.

Kaso m.

This name is found in OB and OW and in the place-name Tregasso.

Kasreth m.

Cornish version of the OW name of Cadreith. See also **Kasretha**.

Kasretha f.

A feminine form of the above name.

Kasvelyn m.

Found in the great Cornish language play **Bywnans Meryasek**. This heroic name is derived from the British *catu-belinos* and means 'fine war, battle'.

Kaswal m.

Cornish version of the strong name from OW. **Kaswal** is found, combined with **ros** 'heath, hill-spur', in the place-name Rosecadgewell. It has the meaning 'battle powerful'.

Kaswallon m.

From OW and found in the ancient Cornish place-name *hryt catwallon*.

Kasworon m.

This great Cornish name, from OC, means 'battle hero'.

Kasworan m.

According to Gover this name is found in the place-name Tregajorran.

Kaswynn m.

This great sounding name is derived from British *catu-uindos* and means 'fair battle'. See also **Kaswynna**.

Kaswynna f.

A strong name for a girl form of the above name.

Kaswyth m.

Not to be confused with **kaswydh** 'a thicket', this name is from OW and found in the place-name Tregaswith.

Katell f.

This is a Cornish equivalent to English Katherine and Breton Katell.

Kathik f.

This lovely name in **Kernewek** means 'kitten'.

Ke m.

He was a friend of **Fili** and of **Gildas** who wrote a history of the Angle, Saxon and Jutish invasions of Britain. **Ke** tried to make peace between **Arthur** and **Mordred** and is mentioned as being **Arthur's** steward according to *The Three Stout Swineherds of the Island of Britain*. His feast day is 3rd October. See **Gildas**.

Kebi m.

This saint was born in Cornwall but went to Ireland and then established a monastery in North Wales. **Kebi** is remembered at **Dewlogh**/Duloe and **Trerigni**/Tregoney. His feast day is 12th December.

Kelest m.

This name is from OC and found in the place-name Tregellas near **Lannbroboes**/Probus and is found as *Tref celest* in an ancient land charter that pre-dates the Domesday Book. (**trev** is another form of **tre** 'settlement, farm')

Kelli f.

From **Kernewek**, meaning 'grove' but is pronounced the same as the girls' name Kelly. This is Irish, being derived from Ceallaigh, 'descendant of Ceallach'.

Kelynn f.

This name in **Kernewek** means 'holly' and so is an equivalent to the name Holly.

Kenbris m.

This name is found in all three of the British languages; in OB as Conbrit, in OW as Cynbryd as well as in OC.

Kendal m.

This mysterious Celtic name is found in the place-name Tregondal.

Kendalan m.

According to Gover this name is found in the place-name Tregantallan.

Kendern m.

This name is from OW and may be found in the place-name Linkindale. **Kendern** means 'chief lord'.

Kendhelik m.

Cornish version of the Welsh name Cynddylig. **Kendhelik** is mentioned in the Welsh triad of *Kulhwch and Olwen*.

Kendives m.

This name is found in the place-name Tregongeeves near **Sen Ostell**/St. Austell.

Keneder m.

A name found in all three British languages OB, OC and OW and also in the place-name Tregender. **Keneder** has the meaning 'bold chief'.

Kenek m.

This name is found in the Cornish place-name Boconnoc which is derived from **bos** 'dwelling' + **Kenek**.

Kenfi m.

A pioneer farmer with a Welsh name and found in the place-name Biscovey.

Kengi m.

This name is from OW and may be found in the place-name Treginey.

Kenhedhow m.

Another name from OW and found in the place-name Tregonetha.

Kenhel m.

From both OB and OW and found in the place-name Boskennal. **Kenhel** has the meaning 'generous chief'. See also **Konhel** and **Kenhela**.

Kenhela f.

A feminine form of the above name.

Kenhi m.

From OB and OC and found in the North Cornwall place-name Bossiney.

Kenlas m

Cornish version of the Welsh name Cynlas. **Kenlas** was the 6th century king criticised by Gildas.

Kennega f.

A Cornish feminine form of the name below.

Kennek m.

The name of the man who owned or built Castle Canyke at **Bosvenegh**/Bodmin. The **Kernewek** version of the name is **Kastell Kennek**. See also **Kennega**. Gwas Kennek is the bardic name of **Graham Sandercock**, the Chair of **Kesva an Taves Kernewek**.

Kennerth m.

From **Gerlyver Meur** this name in **Kernewek** means 'encouragement'.

Kenneves m.

This name is found in the place-name Bosneives.

Kennon m.

From both our sister languages, OB and OW, and found in the place-name Boskednan.

Kenow m.

From OW and found in the place-name Tregenna. **Kenow** means 'cub'. Tregenna Castle Hotel was the venue of the 1997 International Celtic Film Festival.

Kensi f.

This is the name of the river near **Lannstefan**/Launceston. The <-i> shows it is a Celtic river-name but its precise meaning is lost.

Kenvel m.

Cornish equivalent for the Breton Konvael and means 'princely chief'.

Kenver m.

From OW and found in the place-name Boskenver. **Kenver Easten** was the drummer with Cornish rock band **The Way** who performed in both English and Cornish. See also **Kenvera**.

Kenvera f.
A feminine form of the above name.

Kenwal m.
According to Gover this name is from OW and found in the place-name Tregonwall.

Kenwynn m.
From OW and found combined with **bos** 'dwelling' in the place-name Boskenwyn.

Kenwythen m.
This great name comes from OB and OW and has the meaning 'high battle'.

Kenwys m.
A good sounding name from OW and found in the place-name Langunnet.

Kerdhin m.
From **Gerlyver Meur** this name in **Kernewek** means 'rowan'.

Kerdhinenn f.
Also from **Gerlyver Meur** this name in **Kernewek** means 'rowan tree'.

Kerenn f.
This also means 'rowan tree' but is a shortened form of **Kerdhinenn**. **Kerenn** is the bardic name of the Cornish folklorist and writer **Kathleen Hawke**.

Kerghydh m.
Meaning 'heron' this is the bardic name of **Wella Herring**, the first person to teach the Cornish language as part of the school curriculum.

Kerensa f.
This means 'love' and has already gained some popularity as a girl's name in Cornwall.

Keresenn f.
Kernewek gives us this name which means 'cherry'.

Keresik m.

From OW and found in the place-name Tregerrick. **Keresik** in **Kernewek** means 'darling, loved one'.

Keri f.

She is patron of **Egloskeri**/Egloskerry near Launceston and was one of the 24 children of King Brychan.

Kerra f.

This name in **Kernewek** means 'dearer'.

Kerrys m.

A name from OW and found in **Lyskerrys**/Liskeard.

Kerwys m.

Gover states that this name is from OW and found in the place-name Nankervis. The name may simply be the **Kernewek** word **kerwys** 'stags' as found in **Lyskerrys**/Liskeard.

Keryek m.

Another mysterious Celtic name found in the Cornish place-name of Tregerrick.

Keryen m.

This name is from OB and found in the place-name Tregerrin. See also **Keryena**.

Keryena f.

A Cornish feminine form of the above name.

Keski m.

From OW and found in the Cornish place-name Tregiskey.

Kessena f.

This is the feminine form of **Kesson**.

Kessenyans m.
This name in **Kernewek** and has the lovely meaning of 'harmony'.

Kesson m.
This name in modern **Kernewek** means 'harmonious'.

Kest m.
A very Cornish name from the OC period and found in the place-name Lankeast.

Kestenenn f.
In **Kernewek** this name means 'chestnut tree'. It is also the bardic name of **Morwenna Jenkin** who holds the Celtic Studies Chair at the University of Brest, Brittany.

Kevardhu m. or f.
This would make a great name for a baby born in December.

Kevelek m.
Another name from a pioneer farmer found in OW and as Keveleg in Breton. It is also found in the Cornish place-name Biscovellet. **Kevelek** in **Kernewek** means 'woodcock'.

Kevern m.
This is a name taken from the English version of **Lannaghevran** – St. Keverne. According to Bice this has been used as a Christian name before. See **Aghevran**.

Kevrin m.
This name in **Kernewek** means 'mystery, secret'.

Kevrina f.
This is a feminine form of the above name; **Kevrin**.

Kevyl m.
This name is from OW and is found in the place-name Nanskeval and may have the meaning of 'horse'.

Keyna f.

She was one of the 24 children of Brychan and has a village and holy well named after her. The well is said to give dominance to the first of a newly-wed couple to drink the water. Her feast day is the 8th of October.

Kewera f.

This name in modern **Kernewek** means 'fulfilment'.

Kewrys m.

Gover says this a name from OW and found in the place-name Tregowris. However Padel believes it is **kowrys** 'hallow ford'.

Kian m.

Another name is from OW and found in the place-name Tregian.

Klara f.

This is a Cornish equivalent of Breton Klara and English Claire or Clare.

Kleder m.

His church is to be found at **Sen Kleder**/St. Clether near **Lannstefan**/Launceston and he was one of the 24 children of King Brychan of Wales.

Klemmo m.

Cornish equivalent for Clement or Clemence. The Cornwall Subsidies of 1543 record a *Clemow Peris* of **Lannsiek**/St. Just in Roseland.

Klemmens m.

This was a common surname in **Kernow**/Cornwall in the Middle Ages. In the Cornwall Military Survey and Subsidies Roll there were a *Clemens Saundry* and a *Clemens Treveldris* of **Egloswendron**/Wendon and a *Clemens Carasker* of **Hellys**/Helston.

Kler m.

A saint came from England to Cornwall in the 8th century. He has his church at **Sen Kler**/St. Cleer, near **Lyskerrys**/Liskeard. **Kler** was pursued by a local chieftainess, who fell in love with him, but he snubbed her and ran away. She was so enraged that she had him murdered. His feast day is 4th November.

Klesek m.

This name comes via OC and OW from British **kluto* and means 'famous'.

Klodri m.

A name which is from OW and may be found in the place-name Nancledra, the local pronunciation of which is 'Cledry'.

Klosek m.

This name is from OW and found in the place-name Treglossack.

Klusno m.

Another Welsh name but found in Cornwall in the place-name Treglines.

Klust m.

A Welsh name respelled in **Kernewek** from the Arthurian triad of *Kulhogh and Olwen*. He could hear an ant 50 miles away!

Koben m.

This mysterious name may be found in the place-name Boscobban.

Koesvoren f.

This was a bardic name with the meaning 'wood nymph'.

Kogwethyen m.

According to Gover this name is found in the place-name Lanwithan. See also **Gwethyen**.

Kolan m.

His church is to be found at the village bearing his name, three miles east of **Tewynn Bleustra**/Newquay. **Kolan**'s feast day is on 20th May.

Kolenn m.

This name is from both OB and OW and found in the place-name Tregulland.

Kollenn f.

In **Kernewek** means 'hazel tree' and so is an equivalent to the English Hazel.

Kolomm m.

Equivalent of the Scottish male names Calum and Malcolm and the Irish Colm. The name means 'dove'. In Cornwall the name has been recorded as female, see **Kolomma**.

Kolomma f.

The name means 'dove' and, in Cornwall, the patron saint of St. Columb Major and St. Columb Minor is definitely female. She was pursued by a pagan chieftain and refused to renounce her faith. He had her beheaded at **Rudhfos**/Ruthvos which is derived from **rudh** 'red' + **fos** 'wall or bank'. Some say the name refers to **Kolomma's** martyrdom but others, being less romantic, say the name refers to the red manganese deposits in the area. See **Kolomm** for the male version of this name.

Kolonnek m.

This name in **Kernewek** means 'hero' and is derived from **kolonn** 'heart' and not **kolon** meaning 'bowel'.

Kolonnoges f.

This name in **Kernewek** means 'heroine'. See also **Kolonnek**.

Kolyn m.

In **Kernewek** this name means 'puppy' but it is pronounced the same way as the English name Colin.

Kommolenn f.

Kernewek gives us this girl's name that means 'cloud'.

Kon m. or f.

Eglosverther/Merther marks the spot where this mysterious Celtic saint met his end.

Konan m.

This saint has his church at Washaway near **Ponsrys**/Wadebridge. **Konan's** feast day is 23rd July. **Konan** was the name of the Cornish Bishop at the time of the Athelstan massacres. The personal name is also found in Tregonning.

Konani m.

The name of the Breton King in the Cornish language play **Bywnans Meryasek**. Here he introduces himself;

Gelwys yzof conani	**Gelwys yth ov Konani,**
Mytern yn bryton vyan	**Myghtern yn Breten Vyghan**
Han gvlascor pur yredy	**Ha'n gwlaskor pur yredi**
Me a bev ol yn tyan	**My a biw oll yn tien**
Der avys ov arlyzy	**Der avis ow arlydhi**
Mones y fannaf lemmyn	**mones y fannav lemmyn**
the duk pen an chevalry	**dhe dhug penn an chevalri**
Nesse zymmo yn certan	**nessa dhymmo yn sertan**
Par del yv ef.	**par deli yw ev.**

I am called Conany, / King of Brittany / and the kingdom right and readily / I possess altogether. / By advice of my lords / I will go now / to the Duke, head of chivalry, / Next to me certainly / as he is.

Konbris m.

From our sister language, Breton and found in the place-name Degembris.

Konega f.

A feminine form of the name below.

Konek m.

Found in both OB and OW and found in the place-names Tregunnick and Boconnoc. See also **Konega**.

Kones m.

This name is from OB and OW and found in the place-name Tregonnet.

Kongar m.

A saint that has his church at **Lanneves**/Lanivet, near **Bosvenegh**/Bodmin. **Kongar** also appears as a personal name in Tregonger.

Kongen m.

Another name from a pioneer farmer **Kongen** is from OB and found in the place-name Tregonian.

Kongwithen m.

A name from both OB and OW and found in the Cornish place-name Tregwethin.

Konhebris m.

According to Gover this name is from OW and found in the place-name Tregonebris.

Konhel m.

From OB and found in the place-name Boskennal. See also **Konhela**.

Konhela f.

A feminine form of the above name.

Konin m.

When I'd been cheeky my mother used to call me a rabbit. **Konin** in **Kernewek** means 'rabbit'.

Konogan m.

This name is from OW and may be found in the place-name Tregongon.

Konor m.

An Irish name Conchobas meaning 'high desire'. The name was brought to Cornwall in the age of Saints and gave rise to **Goengonor**/Conner Downs near **Heyl**/Hayle. Indeed the whole of County Penwith was known as Connerton in the Domesday Book. The ancient manor of Connerton was swallowed by the shifting sands of St. Ives Bay.

Konwenna f.

The name of the daughter of an ancient Cornish ruler.

Korentin m.

A Celtic saint that is honoured at Cury near **Hellys**/Helston.

Kornelli m.

A name found at Cornelly near **Trerini**/Tregoney. The Breton version of this name is Korneli.

Korrek m.

A name found in the place-name Tregorrick near **Sen Ostell**/St. Austell. This name is not to be confused with **korrik** 'dwarf'.

Kostentin m.

According to an ancient Scottish manuscript, **Kostentin** or Constantine was a Cornish king , bearing a Roman name. He abdicated when his wife died and was then converted by St. Petroc. **Kostentin** left for Ireland to become a monk. His true identity was revealed and he joined Colmcille in Scotland. It is said that he became Scotland's first martyr. In Cornwall, he gave his name to **Lanngostentin**/Constantine and **Porthkostentin**/Constantine Bay, near **Lannwedhenek**/Padstow.

Kowann f.

A modern name that would suit a wide eyed baby, the meaning being 'owl'.

Koweth m.

This friendly name in **Kernewek** means 'friend'.

Kowethes f.

This is the feminine version of **Koweth** and also means 'friend'.

Kowses m.

This name, from **Gerlyver Meur**, means 'conscience, conviction'.

Kowydh m.

From OW and found in the Cornish place-name Tregoweth.

Kres m.

This name in modern **Kernewek** means 'peace'. It is also the cry of the Gorsedd. The Grand Bard asks three times is there peace? All the assembled bards answer "**Kres!**"

> **Unnweyth y hwovynnav orthowgh hwi Eus kres?**
> **Kres!**
> **Diwweyth y hwovynnav orthowgh hwi Eus kres?**
> **Kres!**
> **Teyrweyth y hwovynnav orthowgh hwi Eus kres?**
> **Kres!**

Kres f.

Although spelt like the above this name is feminine. **Kres** in **Kernewek** means 'faith' and so is an equivalent of English Faith.

Kresa f.

A feminine form of **Kres** and also means 'peace'.

Krida f.

Little is known of this mysterious Celtic saint but she has her church at **Krida**/Creed, 6 miles west of **Sen Ostell**/St. Austell.

Krowenna f.

She gave her name to **Egloskrowenna**/Crowan, near **Kammbronn**/Camborne.

Kubert m.

This saint was of noble birth from Wales. His name is found with **Karensek** and **Briek**, the three being venerated in Wales, Brittany and Cornwall. In the 14th century he became confused with the English St. Cuthbert of Lindisfarne.

Kudhon f.

This name in **Kernewek** and from **Gerlyver Meur** means 'wood pigeon'.

Kudynn m.

This name is found in the Cornish place-name of Tregidden from **tre** 'farm, settlement' + **Kudynn**.

Kughyen m.

A very mysterious name found in the place-name Tregiffian.

Kuhelyn m.

A name from both OB and OW and found in the Cornish place-name Tregullan.

Kynhorn m.

Another name is from both OB and OW and found in the place-names **Pollkynhorn**/Polkinghorne and **Lanngynhorn**/Linkinhorne.

Kyni m.

This name is found in the Cornish place-name Bossiney which is derived from **bos** 'dwelling' **+ Kyni**. Bossiney Books is a Cornish based publisher.

Kynilik m.

This name is from OW and found in the place-name Trenilk.

Kynsa m. or f.

A name in **Kernewek** that means 'first' and would be a great name for an eldest child.

Kyswynn m.

According to Gover this name is from OW and may be found in the place-name Tregisswyn.

Kytta f.

A feminized version of the name below and thus an equivalent to Christina.

Kytto m.

Cornish version of Christopher as well as a Cornish family-name.

Kywa f.

She is remembered at **Lanndogho**/St. Kew and was believed to have been the sister of **Dogho**. Her feast day is 8th February.

Kywni f.

In **Kernewek** this means 'moss' but in dialect has come to mean 'mould, litchen, moss'.

Lagasek m.

This name in **Kernewek** means 'big eyed'. See also **Kowann**.

Lallow m.

A chapel at **Mahunyes**/Menheniot was dedicated to St. Lalluwy whose name was *Lallow* in 1500.

Lasek f.

She is only remembered by her church and holy well at **Egloslasek**/Ladock, near **Truru**/Truro.

Lelder f.

Meaning 'loyalty' in **Kernewek** this has been used as a bardic name.

Lerryn f.

The Irish name Clodagh, in Gaelic now spelt Clóda, is derived from the River Clóideach. Similarly the Cornish River Lerryn gives us this beautiful girl's name.

Lesik m.

This name is found in the Cornish place-name of Trelissick.

Leven m.

Although there is a parish St. Leven, this is in fact dedicated to St. Selevan. **Leven** means 'smooth' and is also a river-name. Porthleven is derived from **porth** 'cove harbour' + **leven** 'smooth flowing stream'. See also **Seleven** and **Levena**.

Levena f.

A feminine form of the above name that gives us this beautiful name.

Leveni f.

The Irish name Clodagh is derived from the River Clóideach. Similarly the Cornish river-name of **Leveni**/Lovenny gives us this name which means 'smooth flowing river'.

Lew m.

Cornish version of English Leo. This name is from all three British languages OB, OC and OW meaning 'lion'. **Lew** is also found in the place-name Trelew.

Lewedh m.

From OW and found in the place-names Treloeth and Trelow. The mixture of <th> and nothing shows this name has a <dh> and not a <th>.

Lewhel m.

Nothing is known of this name except that it is found in the place-name Bollowall.

Lewik m.

Using the –ik suffix this name in **Kernewek** means 'lion cub'.

Lewyan m.

Gover states that this name is found in the place-name Trelowia.

Livri m.

This name is found in the Cornish place-name **Lannlivri**/Lanlivery in Mid Cornwall which is derived from **lann** 'enclosure' + **Livri**.

Loergann f.

In **Kernewek** this name has the romantic meaning of 'moonlight'.

Loes m.

Equivalent of Welsh Llwyd and the Anglicized Lloyd.

Lokryn m.

Bice says that this was not an uncommon name in pre 18th century Cornwall.

Los m.

In the Arthurian triads he was the brother-in-law of **Arthur**.

Lowdhas m.

This personal name comes from OC and OW.

Lowen m.

This name in modern **Kernewek** means 'happy'. **Lowen** may also be found in the place-name Burlawn.

Lowena f.

The **Kernewek** word for 'happiness, joy' and hence an equivalent to Joy. The Cornish dialect expert **Joy Stephenson** wrote a magazine column under the name **Maid Lowena**.

Lowenek f.

Using the **–ek** suffix 'abounding in' this name in **Kernewek** means 'joyful'.

Lowenna f.

This name from **Kernewek** means 'happier'.

Lowydhenn f.

This lovely sounding name has the meaning 'laurel tree' and has been used as a bardic name.

Luga m.

This name is found in the Cornish place-name Treligga which is derived from **tre** 'farm, settlement' + **Luga**.

Lughesenn f.

In modern **Kernewek** means 'lightening flash'. This name has the same root as French Lucille.

Luk m.

Cornish version of the Biblical name Luke.

Lun m.

This would be a good name for a boy born on Monday. **Dy'Lun** is **Kernewek** for Monday.

Lybyan m.

In the Cornwall Subsidies for 1524 a *Lybyan Bryton*, alien recorded as living in **Egloswendron**/Wendron. See also **Lybyana**.

Lybyana f.

A lovely feminine name form of the above name.

Lyw m.

Meaning 'ruler' this name is found in OW as *Lleu*. In **Kernewek** the verb **lywya** means 'to steer, to direct'.

Lywader m.

This mysterious name is found in the place-name Trelawder and its meaning may be 'steersman, ruler'.

Lywargh m.

According to Bice this name comes from OC and OW.

Lywydh m.

This OC name means 'ruler'. See also **Lyw**.

Mab m.

This name is found in the Cornish place-name **Lannvab**/Mabe, *Lavabe* 1524.

Mabli f.

Equivalent of English Mabel and Welsh Mabli.

Mabon f.

This saint was one of the 24 children of Brychan. She is patron of **Sen Mabon**/St. Mabyn, near **Ponsrys**/Wadebridge and appears in the windows of St. Neot's church. Her feast day is the 18th of November.

Madern m.

He is remembered at **Eglosvadern**/Madron, near **Pennsans**/Penzance and has the most famous holy well in Cornwall. His feast day is celebrated on 17th May. Also in the Cornwall Military Survey of 1522, this name is recorded as a Christian name, *Maddern Cosyn*.

Mali f.

Equivalent of English Molly and Welsh Mali.

Margh m.

A Cornish form of Mark. In **Kernewek** this name means 'horse'. **Margh** is found in many place-names such as **Karnmargh**/Carn Marth and **Trevargh**/Tremare. See also **Mark**.

Marghell m.

He was featured in the Arthurian triad of *The Three Stout Swineherds of the Island of Britain*.

Mari f.

This is another Cornish form of Mary. **Mari** is one of the characters featured in the weekly **Kernewek** Column in the Western Morning News.

Maria f.

Cornish version of Breton Maria, French Marie and English Mary. See also **Marya**.

Mark m.

Same as English Mark and Welsh Marc. **Mark** is a later form of **Margh**. See also **Margh**.

Marth m.

From **Gerlyver Meur** this name in **Kernewek** means 'wonder'.

Marya f.

Another form of **Maria**, an equivalent to English Mary. See also **Maria**.

Masega f.

A Cornish feminine form of the name below.

Masek m.

This name comes from OC and has the OW equivalent of Madog. **Masek** occurs in the Cornish place-names of **Pollmasek**/Polmassick in Mid Cornwall and **Koesmasek**/Cutmadoc in East Cornwall. See also **Masega**.

Massen m.

This name is derived from Latin Maximus and evolved into Welsh Macsen. **Massen** is the name of a king in the Cornish language play **Bywnans Meryasek** written in 1504.

Mathi m.

A Cornish equivalent of Matthew or Matt. The Cornish language broadcaster and songwriter Matthew Clarke uses **Mathi** when he writes in **Kernewek.**

Medyr m.

A Welsh name found in the Arthurian triad of *Kulhogh and Olwen* he could shoot an arrow between the legs of a wren.

Mel m.

This sweet name in **Kernewek** means 'honey'.

Melder f.

This name in **Kernewek** means 'sweetness' and is based on **mel** meaning 'honey'.

Melek f.

Another name based on the **Kernewek** word **mel,** this time meaning 'sweetness'.

Meler m.

He is honoured at **Ponsnowydh**/Mylor Bridge, near **Aberfal**/Falmouth. The Cornish form is derived from **pons** 'bridge' + **nowydh** 'new'. **Meler** was a Cornish prince who, as a young boy, had his right hand and left foot cut off to stop him using a sword and riding a horse. He had silver ones fitted and miraculously they grew with him! The Cornwall Subsidies of 1524 record a *Milor Pascow* of **Sen Meler**/Mylor parish.

Melgas m.

This is the Cornish version of the Welsh name Maelgad and means 'battle prince'.

Melgi m.

This name is found in the Cornish place-name Trevalga which is derived from **tre** 'farm, settlement' + **Melgi**.

Mellena f.

The Cornwall Subsidies of 1544 record *Mellena Harvy and Mellena Webbe* both of **Lanngynhorn**/Linkinhorne.

Melsa m.

This is the personal name contained in the place-name Demelza of St. Wenn parish. The place-name actually contains **din** 'hill-fort'.

Melskoes m.

This name means 'prince shield' and is found in family-name Trevaskis. See also **Melskoesa**.

Melskoesa f.

A Cornish feminine form of the above name.

Melwas m.

In the Arthurian triads he took **Gwynniver** away with him. **Melwas** is also the equivalent of the Welsh name Maelwas and has the meaning of 'youth prince'.

Melwynn f.

This name in **Kernewek** means 'white fair honey' and would make a great name for a baby with honey coloured hair.

Melyan m.

His name is remembered at **Sen Melyan**/St. Mellion, near **Kelliwik**/Callington and **Eglosvelyan**/Mullion, near **Hellys**/Helston.

Melyn m.

This was the name of **Gyllow** or **Gwyllek's** brother who beheaded the saint. **Melyn** also means 'yellow' in **Kernewek** and so this may be a nickname for someone with yellow hair.

Melynek f.

It means 'green finch' and is listed as a masculine noun in **Gerlyver Meur** but **Liz Carne,** a language bard from **Tewynn Bleustra**/Newquay has made it her bardic name.

Melyonenn f.

This name in modern **Kernewek** means 'violet flower' and so is an equivalent for Violet.

Melys m.

This name is found in the Cornish place-name Trevellas which is derived from **tre** 'farm, settlement' + **Melys**.

Menvra f.

She is one of the 24 children of Brychan. Her church is found at **Sen Menvra**/St. Minver, near **Ponsrys**/Wadebridge. She is known for throwing her comb at the devil. **Menvra**'s feast day is 24th November.

Merdhin m.

This is the **Kernewek** form of Merlin, **Arthur's** magician. However the name is derived from **mor** 'sea' and **din** 'fort' and so simply means 'seafort'. Perhaps Merlin took his name from his castle – which must have been on the coast. Compare the Welsh Myrddin as found in Caerfyrddin/Carmarthen. **Jowann Richards** wrote a comic short story about him; **An Gwiryonedh yn kever Merdhin**. See also **Merdhina**.

Merdhina f.

A Cornish feminine form of the above name.

Meren m.

This saint's name is found at **Sen Meren**/St. Merryn. See **Merina**.

Mergas m.

This name is a Cornish equivalent for the Breton Morgad and means 'great battle'.

Mergher m.

This would make a great name for a boy born on a Wednesday. **Dy'Mergher** is **Kernewek** for Wednesday but **Mergher** means 'Mercury'. See **Merghera**.

Merghera f.

This is a feminine version of the above. Remember the stress falls on the middle syllable; mergh-ER-a.

Merghyon m.

He was the father of **Mark**. See **Margh** and **Mark**.

Merina f.

There is some confusion with the female saint Marina but **Merina** has a different feast day of the 7th of July and is known in Wales at Llanferin and Bodferin. The saint may have been a male or female. See also **Meren**.

Merteryana f.

She is the patron of Forrabury church at **Trevenydh**/Trevena, near **Dintagell**/Tintagell. Her feast day is 9th April.

Mervel m.

This is the Cornish version of the Welsh name Morfael and means 'great prince'.

Meryasek m.

He came from Brittany and founded his church at **Kammbronn**/Camborne. His life is told in the Cornish language play **Bywnans Meryasek**, written in 1504 – the only complete life history of a Saint surviving in Britain.

Beneth du zys meryasek	**Bennath Dyw dhis, Meryasek!**
Pup vr ty yv colonnek	**Pub eur ty yw kolonnek**
Parys rag dysky dader	**parys rag dyski dader**
Meseger scon alemma	**Messejer, skon alemma**
Kegy gans ov mab kerra	**ke jy gans ow mab kerra**
Bys yn mester a grammer	**bys yn mester a ramer.**

God's blessing to you, Meryasek! / Always you are hearty, / Ready to learn goodness. / Messenger, forthwith hence / Go thou with my dearest son / unto the master of grammar.

Meryen m.

This name comes from OB and OW.

Metheven f.

In **Kernewek** this means 'June month' and so is an equivalent to the English name June.

Meurth m.

This can mean the month of March, Tuesday or the planet Mars. Strictly these are **mis-Meurth**, **dy'Meurth** and **Meurth** in **Kernewek**. See also **Meurtha**.

Meurtha f.

This is a feminine form of the above name.

Meva m.

His name is found in Mevagissey which derives from S. Meva + **hag** 'and' S. Isi. See **Mevan** and **Mewan**.

Mevan m.

This may be a form of **Meva** or **Mewan**. See **Mewan**.

Mewan m.

He is said to be the friend and godfather of **Ostell**. Water that he had blessed was believed to have cured skin diseases. He foretold his own death and his corpse did not decay for many years until **Ostell** died. The feast day of **Mewan** is the 21st of June – the summer solstice. The name is also contained in the family name Tremewan.

Mewbres m.

Nothing is known of this saint apart from his patronage of the church at **Kardhinan**/Cardinham and appearing in the windows of St. Neot's church next to Mabon.

Mighal m.

The Cornish for Breton Mikaël, French Michel and English Michael. Edward Lhuyd spelled the Cornish name; *Mîhal,* in 1700. This clearly shows that the first vowel sound is the same as English <ee> written as <i> in **Kernewek**. **Henry Jenner**, the first **Bardh Meur** of **Gorsedh Kernow**, had the bardic name of **Gwas Mighal** 'servant of Michael'.

Mighala f.

A feminine form of **Mighal** and so an equivalent to Breton Mikaëla, French Michelle and English Micheala.

Milyan m.

This was the name of an ancient Cornish ruler and is also found in the Bodmin Manumissions. This name may be a variant of **Melyan**. See **Melyan**.

Milyek m.

According to Bice this name comes from OC and may be from Latin Aemiliacus.

Mindu f.

Using **min** 'face, snout' this name in **Kernewek** means 'swarthy'.

Minhwarth m.

This name from **Kernewek** simply means 'smile'.

Mo f.

A name in modern **Kernewek** meaning 'dawn, dusk' and although a masculine noun in **Gerlyver Meur** the name **Mo** can still be an equivalent of Dawn.

Modres m.

This name comes from the Bodmin Manumissions. **Modres** was the nephew of **Arthur** and raided his castle at *Kellwic* in Cornwall. There is also a Tremoddret 'farm, settlement of **Modres**' in mid Cornwall.

Modron f.

The Cornish version of the Welsh name Modron. **Modron** was a Celtic sea goddess.

Molgh f.

Gerlyver Meur gives us this name from **Kernewek** meaning 'song thrush'.

Mordardh m.

This name in **Kernewek** means 'surf'.

Mordros m.

Kernewek gives us this lovely name which means 'sound of the sea'.

Morega f.

A feminine form of the name below .

Morek m.

This name is from OB and found in the place-name Trevorrick. See also **Morega**.

Moren m.

From both OB and OW and found in the place-name Rosemorran.

Morenn f.

A saint who gave her name to **Lannvorenn**/Lamorran. **Morenn** is an OC personal name found in ancient land charter that pre-dates the Domesday Book as *lannmoren*. (**lann** 'holy enclosure')

Morenwynn f.

This name in **Kernewek** means 'fair maid' – not to be confused with a fairmaid – a smoked herring!

Morgan m.

The Cornish is the same as the Breton and Welsh Morgan. The Welsh name is derived from **meur** 'great' and **kan** 'song'. See also **Morgana**.

Morgana f.

A feminine form of the above name.

Morgares f.

Meaning 'sea lover' this is the bardic name of **Val Brokenshire**, an author and language bard from mid Cornwall.

Morgelynn f.

This lovely sounding name in modern **Kernewek** means 'sea holly'.

Morgenna m.

From OW and found in the place-name Tremagenna.

Morgas m.

This name is from OB and found in the place-name Trevorgas.

Morvardh m.

In **Kernewek** this name means 'sea bard' and is the bardic name of the great poet and writer **Charles Causley**.

Morvargh m.

This name in **Kernewek** means 'seahorse'.

Morvel m.

According to Gover this name is from OW and found in the place-name Tremorle.

Morven m.

In the Cornwall Military Survey of 1522 there is a *Morven Britton labourer*. The family-name of *Britton, Bryton, Bretton* etc. was often given to Bretons who came to live here so **Morven** is probably a Breton name in use in Cornwall. See also **Morvena**.

Morvena f.

A feminine form of the above name.

Morveth m.

The Cornwall Subsidies of 1524 record a *Morveth Bretton, age 16, Alien* of **Sen Gwynnyer**/Gwinear Parish. It is probably a Breton name.

Morvoren f.

From **Gerlyver Meur** this name in **Kernewek** means 'mermaid'.

Morwenna f.

She is honoured at Cornwall's most northerly parish **Lannvorwenna**/Morwenstow. There is a Cornish dance team from the area calling themselves **Myrghes Morwenna** 'daughters of Morwenna'. **Morwenna Banks** is a famous television comedian.

Morwennel f.

A name from modern **Kernewek** meaning 'tern'. **Morwennel** has the literal meaning 'sea swallow'.

Mowgan m.

This Welsh saint has two dedications in Cornwall; **Sen Mowgan yn Peder**/Mawgan-in-Pydar, near **Tewynn Bleustra**/Newquay and **Sen Mowgan yn Managhan**/Mawgan-in-Meneage, near **Hellys**/Helston. 24th of September is his feast day.

Mownan m.

He is remembered at the church just outside the village of **Mownan an Gov**/Mawnan Smith, near **Aberfal**/Falmouth. The lych gate at his church bears the inscription;

> *Da thym ythyu nessa the Thu*
> **Da dhymm yth yw nesa dhe Dhyw**
> It is good for me to approach God

Mowsedh m.

He is remembered at Le Maudez and Lanmodez in his native Brittany and at **Lannvowsedh**/St. Mawes on Cornwall's south coast. 18th November is his feast day.

Myjenn f.

A name from **Kernewek** meaning 'mite, small thing'.

Mynnenn f.

Another name from **Kernewek** that means 'little kid, baby goat'.

Nadeliga f.

A feminine form of **Nadelik** and an equivalent to the feminine Noel.

Nadelik m.

This name in **Kernewek** means 'Christmas' and so is equivalent to Breton Nadeleg, French Noël and English Noel.

Nennys m.

This name is found in the Cornish place-name **Plywnennys**/Pelynt in South east Cornwall which is derived from **plyw** 'parish' + **Nennys**. He is also known at Eglwys Nynnid in Wales.

Nerth m.

A nick name in earlier times; **nerth** in **Kernewek** means 'power'.

Nerthek f.

This name in **Kernewek** means 'powerful'. This may also have been a Cornish nickname.

Nessa m. or f.

A great name for a second born child in **Kernewek** meaning 'second'.

Nestek m.

This name is found in the place-name Lanescot – nothing to do with a lane or a cot!

Neves m.

A name that derives from the British *nemeto-* 'sacred grove' and is found as a personal name in **Lanneves**/Lanivet, near **Bosvenegh**/Bodmin (combined with **lann** 'holy enclosure') and in Carnivas (combined with **karn** 'rock-pile'). **Neves** is also found in OW. See also **Nevesek** and **Nevesa**.

Nevesa f.

A Cornish feminine form of the above name.

Nevesek m.

Deriving from British *nemetaco-*, this name means 'place of holy groves' and is found in the place-name Trenovissick. See also **Neves**.

Neythen m.

This is the Cornish form of the Irish Nectan. See also **Nyghtan**.

Niet m.

A Cornish saint who studied at **Ynyswedrenn**/Glastonbury and returned to Cornwall to become a hermit. He is remembered at **Sen Niet**/St. Neot. **Niet's** relics were stolen by the Saxon King Edgar and the Bishop of Ely and removed to Eynesbury where the English monks founded the new town of St. Neots. His feast day is 31 July. The church is dedicated to a mysterious Celtic saint, see **Gweryr**.

Niwlin f.

She is remembered in the name of **Eglosniwlin**/Newlyn East, near **Tewynn Bleustra**/Newquay. The 'East', in the English form, was added to distinguish it from Newlyn in West Cornwall. Newlyn is derived from **lu** 'army, host' + **lynn** 'pool' and has the Cornish form **Lulynn**. **Niwlin** sailed, with her companion, to Brittany on a leaf!

Nonn f.

She was the mother of Saint David of Wales or Dewi Sant and she is remembered at **Alternonn**/Altarnun, near **Lannstefan**/Launceston. Her feast day is the 15th June.

Nowmel m.

In the Cornwall Subsidies for 1524 a *Nawemeyle Britton* is recorded as living in **Sen Pawl**/Paul.

Nowyen m.

This name is found in the Cornish place-name Trenewan which is derived from **tre** 'farm, settlement' + **Nowyen**.

Nyghtan m.

He was the eldest son of the 24 children of Brychan and his name is found at St. Nectan's Glen, near **Dintagell**/Tintagell and at St. Nectan's Kieve, a waterfall under which he is supposed to be buried. He was beheaded by cattle thieves. His feast day is 17th of June.

Nykka m.

This is a Cornish pet form of Nicholas, Nick etc. See also **Nykklys**.

Nykklys m.

The Cornwall Subsidies record this name as *Nicklys Jane* of **Sen Klemens**/St. Clement Parish in 1543. This is also a pet form of Nicholas. See also **Nykka**.

Nynek m.

From OB and found in the place-name Treninnick.

Nythan m.

This name is from OW and found in the place-name Bosytha and is related to Irish Nechtan.

Odo m.

Also in the Cornwall Military Survey there is a *Odo Jenkin* of **Sen Meler**/Mylor and an *Odo William* of **Eglosheyl**/Egloshayle. **Odo** is a Cornish version of Otto, a Germanic name derived from 'riches'.

Oenes f.

Gerlyver Meur gives us this name which in **Kernewek** means 'ewe lamb'.

Oenik m.

Using the suffix **–ik** this name in **Kernewek** means 'lambkin, little lamb'.

Ojyon m.

This strong name in **Kernewek** means 'ox'.

Olivenn f.

In **Kernewek** means 'olive tree' and so is an equivalent of Olive.

Omfra m.

This is a Cornish pet form of the name Humphrey. See also **Humfra**.

Ors m.

This name in **Kernewek** means 'bear'. This has the same root as **Arthur**, 'bear like'.

Orses f.

This name in **Kernewek** means 'she bear' and shares the same root as **Arthur**.

Osker m.

From OC and found in the place-name Treviscoe recorded in an ancient land charter that pre-dates Domesday as *Tref otcere*.

Ostell m.

Cornish form of the Breton name. **Ostell** founded **Sen Ostell**/St. Austell. He fought off the devil and in the struggle his staff stuck into the ground and turned to stone leaving the Longstone in the playing field of Penrice School.

Owen m.

Cornish equivalent of Welsh Owain based on **Lannowen** – an alternative name for **Egloskubert**/Cubert. In the Cornwall Military Survey of 1522 there is an *Owin Stephyn* of **Lannvorek**/Mevagissey.

Owrek f.

This name in **Kernewek** means 'golden, goldfield'.

Palvan m.

According to Gover this name may be found in the place-name Bospalvans. See also **Palvana**.

Palvana f.

A feminine form of the above name.

Parkyn m.

In the Cornwall Military Survey of 1522 there is a *Parkyn Thoma* recorded as living in the parish of *Uny Redruth,* in the county of *Penwith.*

Pask m.

This name in **Kernewek** means 'Easter' and is constructed on similar line to **Nadelik** and **Nadeliga** for Noel.

Paska f.

One of the feminine forms of **Pask** and **Pasko**.

Paskes f.

Another feminine form of **Pasko** and in **Kernewek** means 'of Easter'.

Paskesow f.

Another feminine form of **Paskow** and in **Kernewek** means 'of Easter'.

Paskow m.

This personal name is found in many old Cornish documents and has the meaning 'of Easter'. In the Cornwall Military Survey of 1522 there are *Pascoe Tregy* of **Lannfiek**/Fiock, *Pascoe Courteys* of **Kardhinan**/Cardinham, and *Pascoe Fyypp* of **Tallann**/Talland amongst many others. This Cornish language name was used even in English speaking areas of Cornwall. It is more familiar to us today as the family name Pascoe.

Pawl m.

Equivalent of Biblical name Paul, Welsh Pawl, Breton Paol, Irish Pól. **Pawl Dunbar** is the Cornish language poet and teacher. See also **Pol.**

Pawli m.

This is a Cornish pet form of Paul and was a common first name in 17th century Cornwall.

Pawlina f.

This is a feminine form of Pawl and equivalent to Breton Paolina and the French and English Pauline.

Pawlyn m.

Bice states that this name comes from OC and may be derived from Latin *Paulinus*.

Peder m.

Equivalent of Welsh Pedr and English Peter. **Peder** was a local chieftain remembered at **Pederwynn Gledh**/North Petherwin and **Pederwynn Dheghow**/South Petherwin in North Cornwall. The –win in the English forms are derived from Cornish **gwynn** meaning 'white or blessed'. **Peder Doherty** is the Cornish speaking bag-piper from **Penndin**/Pendeen. **Peder** is also one of the characters featured in the **Kernewek** Column in the Western Morning News. See also **Pedera**.

Pedera f.

A Cornish feminine form of **Peder** and so an equivalent to the modern English name Petra. See **Peder**.

Pedrega f.

Cornish equivalent of Breton Padriga and French Patricia. See also **Pedrek**.

Pedrek m.

The Cornish version of Patrick. He was a Briton who was captured as a slave and taken to Ireland. The Cornwall Subsidies in 1543 record this name in *Pedrac Mata* in the parish **Lannsiek**/St. Just in Roseland. The final <-ac> shows that the name ends in <-ek> and not <-ig> as in the Welsh and Breton versions of this name. See also **Pedrega**.

Penkast m.

Found only in Late Cornish and may be a shortening of Pentekost. **Penkast** has the meaning 'whitsuntide'.

Pennek m.

Gover says that this name may be found in the place-name Trebinnick. **Pennek** is found in the Bodmin Manumissions and was probably a nickname with the meaning 'big head'.

Pennseviges f.

Also from **Gerlyver Meur** this name in **Kernewek** means 'princess, lady'.

Pennsevik m.

From **Gerlyver Meur** this name in **Kernewek** means 'prince, nobleman'.

Pennwynn m.

This is the Cornish version of the Welsh name Penwyn which means 'white, fair head'.

Peran m.

A variant of Cornwall's patron saint of tinners. See also **Pyran**.

Peredur m.

He is featured in the Arthurian triad of *The Three Knights who kept the Grail*.

Perow m.

In the Cornwall Subsidies for 1545 a *Peraw Peris* is recorded as living in **Sen Leven**/St. Leven.

Peswara m. or f.

This would be a great name for the fourth born child of a family as the name means 'fourth'.

Petrega f.
A feminine form of the name below.

Petrek m.
Petrek has dedications in Wales, Brittany and England as well as Cornwall. He is honoured at **Lannwedhenek**/Padstow. The **Kernewek** form has the name **Gwedhenek**. **Petrek** retired to a hermitage at **Bosvenegh**/Bodmin and his relics were kept there but were stolen in 1177. Henry II had to intervene to recover them for **Bosvenegh**/Bodmin. The personal name is found in Trebetherick and is of OB origin. In the Cornwall Military Survey of 1522 there is a *Petrok Nans* of **Logsulyen**/Luxulyan and a *Petrock Jenkyn* of **Lanneves**/Lanivet. A Latin form is found in 1524; *Petrocus* of **Rysrudh**/Redruth. **Petrok Trelawney** is the well known radio broadcaster. See also **Gwedhenek** and **Petrega**.

Petrok m.
This is an older form of **Petrek**. See **Petrek**.

Piala f.
She was a sister of **Gwynnyer** and gave her name to **Sen Felek**/Phillack, near **Heyl**/Hayle.

Markesen an kuntellyans yw gorfennys. My a wra gyhi!

Pol m.

Equivalent of Biblical name Paul, Welsh Pawl, Breton Paol, Irish Pól. **Pol Hodge** wrote this book. See also **Pawl**.

Polan m.

This name is from OB and may be found in the place-name Trebowland.

Polin f.

A feminine form of **Pol** and so an equivalent to Pauline. **Polin** is the young girl featured in the **Dres an Vlydhen** stories and **Polin Preece** is a Cornish language teacher and playwright.

Predennek m.

In **Kernewek** this means 'British' and Predannack Head near **Lysardh**/The Lizard also has the same meaning.

Proboes m.

He gave his name to **Lannbroboes**/Probus, near Truro and his skull and that of his wife, Grace, are still kept at the church. His feast day is 5th July.

Purek m.

This name may be found in the place-name Treburrick.

Pydannan m.

This name is found in the Cornish place-name Trebudannon which is derived from **tre** 'farm, settlement' + **Pydannon**.

Pynnek m. or f.

A mysterious Celtic saint gave his/her name to **Sen Pynnek**/St. Pinnock near **Lyskerrys**/Liskeard.

Pyra m.

This name is found in the Cornish place-name Polperro which is derived from **poll** 'pool' + **Pyra**.

Pyran m.

The greatest of Cornish saints was in fact an Irishman who floated to **Porthpyran**/Perranporth on a millstone. Amongst many miracles he put the tin into every parish in Cornwall, except **Eglosveryan**/St. Buryan. For this he was made patron saint of tinners – and gave us our national flag. The anglicized version Piran and the local pronunciation with the first syllable as English 'pie' shows that the sound is [I] and so in **Kernewek** written <y>. The form Peran is taken from English historical forms. If you don't know when his feast day is then you're very sad! **Lowender Peran** is Cornwall's great Celtic festival. See also **Peran** and **Pyrana**.

Pyrana f.

A feminine form of the above name.

Pyrk m.

This name is from OB and found in the place-name Treburgie.

Rabas m.

Cornish version of Welsh Robat and English Robert, Rob, Bob, etc. See also **Roparth** and **Rabasa**.

Rabasa f.

A Cornish feminine form of **Rabas** and therefore an equivalent for the English name Roberta. See **Rabas**.

Rannow m.

A name from OB and may be found in the place-name Tranno.

Raw m.

This is a Cornish version of the name Ralph. In the Cornwall Military Survey of 1522 there is a *Raw Thomas* recorded as living in the parish of **Managhan**/Manaccan.

Rawlyn m.

In the Cornwall Subsidies for 1543 a Rawlyn Carpenter of **Pennrynn**/Penryn is recorded.

Redenenn f.

Kernewek gives us this name which means 'fern'.

Renowdyn m.

In the Cornwall Military Survey of 1522 there is a *Renowdyn Nicolas* recorded as living in the parish of **Pyran yn Treth**/Perranzabuloe and armed with a billhook.

Rewan m.

This name is another form of **Ruman**. See **Ruman**.

Reythgi m.

This name may be found in the place-name Bodrifty. It seems to be related to **reyth** 'right, just' and literally means 'justice dog'!

Reydhek m.

This name is from OW and found in the place-name Trevitho in **Eglosvelyan**/Mullion. **Reythek** has the approxiamate meaning of 'abounding in justice'.

Reydhow m.

This name is found in the Cornish place-name Lanreath which is derived from **lann** 'enclosure' + **Reydhow**.

Rigans m.

This Celtic name is found in the place-name Bodrigan and may means 'very royal'. See also **Rigansa**.

Rigansa f.

A Cornish feminine form of the above name.

Rigi m.

Also based on the root meaning 'royal' this name is found in the place-name Bodriggy.

Rigni m.

This name is found in the Cornish place-name Tregoney which is derived from **tre** 'farm, settlement' + **Rigni**.

Rihorn m.

This name is found in **Lannrihorn**/Ruan Lanihorn and means 'royal (man) of iron'.

Riol m.

Found in the Bodmin Manumissions, and may be found in the place-name Rialton. See also **Riola**.

Riola f.

A feminine form of the above name.

Rivelin m.

This name is from OB and may be found in the place-name Boddervarren.

Ris m.

Found in all three British languages, OB, OC and OW. This name is found in the place-name Trefrize. **Ris** is the Cornish equivilent of the common Welsh name of Rhys or Rhees but has nothing to do with the modern **ris** meaning 'rice'!

Riwel m.

The British *rigalis ualos* gave rise to this OB name **Riwel** is also found in the place-name Trerule.

Rojer m.

Cornish spelling of Welsh Rhosier and equivalent of English Roger.

Ronwynn f.

Equivalent of Welsh Rhonwen and English Rowena.

Roparth m.

This is the Cornish equivalent to Breton Roparzh and English Robert.

Rosenn f.

This name in modern **Kernewek** means 'rose' and so is an equivalent for English Rose, Rosy etc. and Breton Rozenn. **Rosenn** is one of the characters featured in the weekly **Kernewek** Column in the Western Morning News.

Rovel m.

This name is from OB and found in the place-names Treravel, Trerovel and Trevoll.

Rowel m.

From OB and found in the place-name Bodrawle.

Ruan m.

He has dedications at **Ruan Veur**/Ruan Major and **Ruan Vyghan**/Ruan Minor, near **Lysardh**/The Lizard and **Lannrihorn**/Ruan Lanihorn on the Fal. He has his feast day on 30th August. See also **Ruana**.

Ruana f.

A Cornish feminine form of the above name.

Rudhega f.

A feminine form of **Rudhek** but still meaning 'robin'.

Rudhek m.

This name in **Kernewek** means 'robin' and so is a good equivalent of Robin – Batman's friend.

Rudhynn m.

This name is found in the Cornish place-name Bedruthan, found on the North Cornish coast, which is derived from **bos** 'dwelling' + **Rudhynn**.

Ruman m.

This name is found in the place-name Treraven. The Cornwall Subsidies record this name as *Roman Pascow* of **Lannfiek**/St. Feock Parish in 1543.
See also **Rewan**.

Ruthan m.

This mysterious name is found in the place-name Bedruthan.

Rychow f.

This was a popular name for girls in 17th century Cornwall.

Rydhses m.

This name in **Kernewek** means 'freedom'. **Rydhses** is written on the back of the **Mighal Yosep an Gov** commemorative T-shirt.

Rywvanes f.

This name in **Kernewek** means 'queen' and so would be an equivalent to Queenie. The more usual word used in speech for queen is **myghternes**.

Sadorn m.

A name from OW and found in the place-name Tresaddern. **Sadorn** is also the Cornish for Saturn the planet. **Dy'Sadorn** is **Kernewek** for Saturday.

Salan m.

This name is derived from the OC of the Bodmin Manumissions and may also be found in the place-name Carsella. See also **Salana**.

Salana f.

A lovely sounding girl's name from of the above. See **Salan**.

Salwys m.

This name is found in the Cornish place-name Lansallos which is derived from **lann** 'enclosure' + **Salwys**.

Samson m.

He is venerated at **Goelnans**/Golant, near **Fowydh**/Fowey and at **Bre Dheghow**/Southill, near **Kellwik**/Callington. **Samson** went on to Brittany and was a founding father of the Breton Church. His feast day is 28th July. The Cornwall Subsidies of 1543 record *Samson Hicke* of **Sen Meren**/St. Merryn.

Samuel m.

This name is from Hebrew via OC and found in the place-name Tresamble.

Sander m.

This is a Celtic pet form of Alexander which gives rise to many different family names such as Sando, Sander, etc. See also **Sandera**.

Sandera f.

A Cornish feminine form of the above name and an equivalent to English Alexandra and Alexis.

Sankres m.

He accidentally killed his father and went away to become a swineherd. **Sankres** is remembered at the church of **Eglossankres**/Sancreed, near **Penn an Wlas**/Lands End.

Sansek m.

Nothing is known of this Celtic name except that it is found in the place-name Carzantick.

Sansel m.

This holy name in **Kernewek** means 'saintly'.

Sansela f.

Using the feminine **–a** suffix this is a feminine form of **Sansel**.

Santo m.

A Cornish pet form of Alexander, Alex etc. See also **Sander**.

Seder m.

This name is from OB and found in the place-name and thus the family-name Tresidder. See also **Sedera**.

Sedera f.

A feminine form of the above name.

Sel m.

From OW and may be found in the place-name Launcells.

Seleven m.

Found in OW and found in the place-name Bosliven in West Cornwall. **Seleven** is also the Cornish form of the Biblical name Solomen. He was the son of **Erbin**, grandson of **Gerens**, brother of **Just** and father of **Kubi**. He is remembered at **Sen Selevan**/St. Levan. The English form confuses him with another Celtic saint. See **Leven**.

Senan m.

He is patron of the most westerly church on the Island of Britain. **Senan's** feast day is held on the 8ᵗʰ of March.

Senara f.

Sen Senara/Zennor, near **Porthia**/St. Ives carries her name but nothing is known of this mysterious Celtic saint. This initial <z> is a fairly recent anglification, Zennor being *Senara* in 1361 and *Sener* 1562. **Senara Wilson** is a Cornish film producer.

Serlo m.

In the Cornwall Military Survey of 1522 there is a *Serlo Betty* recorded as living in the parish of St.Gluvyas and in 1524 the Cornwall Subsidies has a *Serllo Britton, alien* of **Lanngostentin**/Constantine.

Sethik f.

This name in **Kernewek** means 'dart'.

Sevenek m.

A name found in the place-name Tresvennack. Remember there are three syllables and the stress falls on the middle one ie Sev-EN-ek.

Sevienn f.

This delicious name from **Kernewek** means 'strawberry'.

Sevyn m.

From yet another pioneer farmer, a name from OW and may be found in the place-name Nansevan.

Sewena f.

This up-beat name in **Kernewek** means 'success'.

Sewyl m.

According to Gover this name is from OW and found in the place-name Tresawle. **Sewyl** is pronounced with two syllables ie Seu-yl.

Siek m.

A name found in the Cornish name of **Lannsiek**/St. Just in Roseland and also in our sister country of Brittany

Sion m.

This name is from OW and found in the place-name Lanzion and nothing to do with Zion. However Padel believes the place-name is derived from **nans** 'valley' + **syghan** 'dry place'.

Silwynn f.

She was the sister of **Seleven**. See **Seleven**.

Siw f.

An abreviation of the following name and equivalent to Sue.

Siwsann f.

Cornish version of Welsh Siwsann and equivalent of English Susan.

Siwsi f.

A Cornish version of the English Susy.

Skaw m.

A name that means 'elder trees'. It forms the second element in **Treskaw**/Tresco in **Syllan**/The Scilly Isles. See **Skawenn**.

Skawenn f.

This means a 'single elder tree' and has been used as a bardic name. See **Skaw**.

Skilli m.
In the Arthurian triad of *Kulhogh and Olwen* he could run along the tops of trees!

Skorenn f.
A new name which has the meaning 'branch' in **Kernewek**.

Skorrennik m. or f.
In **Kernewek** this means 'little branch' and is a feminine noun so is suitable for a girl's name. **Skorrennik** has also been used as a bardic name for a man and so is also suitable for a boy's name. **Douglas Hyde** who was the first president of Ireland, took this as his bardic name.

Skovarnek m. or f.
From **Gerlyver Meur** this name means 'long eared' or 'hare'.

Sol m.
In the Arthurian triad of *Kulhogh and Olwen* he could stand on one foot all day!

Sowdhan m.
This surprising name in **Kernewek** means 'surprise'.

Splanna f.
A modern female name in **Kernewek** that means 'brighter'.

Splannder m.
Taken from Bice this name in **Kernewek** means 'brightness'.

Stedhyana f.
She is remembered at **Sen Stedhyana**/Stithians, near **Rysrudh**/Redruth.

Stefan m.
The Cornish version of English Stephen, Steven, Steve etc. and Breton Stefan. The **Kernewek** for Launceston is **Lannstefan** 'holy enclosure of St. Stephen'.

Stefana f.

This is a feminine version of **Stefan** and so is a Cornish equivalent for Stephanie.

Sterenn f.

Another lovely name from **Kernewek** that means 'star'. It is also the equivalent for the name Stella.

Sterennik f.

Using the **–ik** suffix this name in **Kernewek** means 'little star'.

Stergann m.

This romantic name in **Kernewek** means 'starlight'. See also **Sterganna**.

Steganna f.

A feminine form of the above name.

Sul m.

This name from **Gerlyver Meur** would be appropriate for a boy born on a Sunday as **dy'Sul** is **Kernewek** for Sunday. See also **Sula**.

Sula f.

This is a feminine form of the above name.

Sulek m.

Found in the place-names Carsullan and Crugsillick. **Krug** is **Kernewek** for burial mound and so **Sulek** must have been a very important man to have his own burial mound.

Sulesek m.

According to Gover this name is from OC and found in the place-name Bosoljack.

Sulgan m.

This name is from OC and found in the place-name Tresilgan and Tresulgan. See also **Sulgana**.

Sulgana f.

A Cornish feminine form of the above name.

Sulgi m.

A name that may mean 'sun dog' and is found in the place-name Causilgey.

Sulwethan m.

Found in the place-name **Tresulwethan**/Treslothan near **Trewoen**/Troon resting place of **John Harris** – Cornwall's greatest poet.

Sulyen m.

His name is found at **Tresulyen**/Tresillian, near **Truru**/Truro and at **Logsulyen**/Luxulyan, near **Bosvenegh**/Bodmin. See also **Sulyena**.

Sulyena f.

A Cornish feminine form of the above name.

Sybella f.

The Cornwall Subsidies record a *Sybella Stapelyn wid.* as resident in the Borough of **Lyskerrys**/Liskeard in 1543. The feminine suffix is missing from *Sybell Tregose wid.* of Anthony – an English speaking area in the 16th century.

Sydhni m.

He has his church at **Sen Sydhni**/Sithney, near **Hellys**/Helston. **Sydhni's** feast day is the 4th of August.

Symon m.

Cornish spelling of Welsh Seimon and equivalent of English Simon.

Sylvester m.

From Latin and found in the ancient Celtic village of Chysauster. This was spelt *Chisalvestre* in 1313 and is derived from **chi** 'house' + **Sylvester**.

Sysela f.

The Cornwall Subsidies record *Sissela* of **Dewlogh**/Duloe in 1544.

Talan m.

This name is from OC and OW and found in the place-name Talland near **Logh**/Looe is derived from **tal** 'hill-brow' + **lann** 'enclosure' and remarkably a saint was invented to fit the place-name – Saint Tallanus! See also **Talana**.

Talana f.

A feminine form of the above name.

Talek m.

A name is from OW and found in the place-name Botallick. **Talek** means 'broad browed' or 'clever' and corresponds to the dialect 'long-headed' clever. **Talek** was the bardic name of **Ernest Retallick Hooper**, Cornwall's third **Bardh Meur** and a founder member of **Mebyon Kernow**.

Talens m.

This name is from OC and found in the place-name Tredellans.

Tallagh m.

He is recorded as being the father of **Tristan**.

Talwynn f.

This beautiful feminine name in modern **Kernewek** means 'fair brow'. A Latin form of this name is found in the Cornwall Subsidies of 1524; *Talwinus Bretton Alien* of **Sen Pawl**/Paul.

Tamara f.

She was the earth spirit that was turned into the River Tamar by her father whilst in a rage. The name is also found in the Bible; the daughter-in-law of Judah and the daughter of King David.

Tamsin f.

Although the most common female Cornish name after **Jenefer,** it is derived from Thomasina, the female form of Thomas. Indeed the Cornwall Subsidies record this name as *Thomasina Tregeer* of **Sen Sydhni**/Sithney and *Tamosyn Saunder* of **Chi war Dreth**/Tywardreath. However the name existed in 1543; *Tamsin Style* of **Sen Menvre**/St. Minver and *Tamsin Bathe* of **Eglostudi**/St. Tudy. **Tamsin Curnow** is a journalist for Packet Newspapers.

Tangi m.

This name is from OB and OW and found in the place-name Polstangey. The Breton version is also Tangi. The Cornwall Subsidies of 1543 records a *Tangy* of **Breanek**/St. Agnes. The literal meaning of **Tangi** is 'fire dog'! This name is also featured in **Tangi** the song on the **Planet Kernow** tape (children's songs in **Kernewek**).

Tanwynn m.

Cornish version of the Welsh feminine name Tanwen which means 'white fire'.

Tanwynna f.

This is the feminine form of the Welsh name Tanwen.

Taran f.

This name in **Kernewek** means 'thunder' and has exactly the same spelling and meaning with the Breton cognate.

Tarow m.

Gerlyver Meur gives us this powerful name which in **Kernewek** means 'bull'.

Tathan m.

This name is from OW and may be found in the place-name Botathan.

Tavi m.

He was a giant who, with his brother **Taw**, courted **Tamara**. When **Tamara** was turned into a river, **Tavi** was heart-broken and asked his father to do the same to him so his waters could mingle with hers for all time. See **Tamara** and **Taw**.

Taw m.

Taw was a giant who was turned into a river so that his waters could mingle with his beloved **Tamara** but was tricked and ended up as the River Taw in Devon, flowing northwards, away from the River Tamar.

Tedha f.

She was one of King Brychan's 24 children and founded the church which bears her name; **Eglostudha**/St. Teath. **Tedha** shares her feast day with the great pagan festival of May Day.

Tegenn f.

This name in **Kernewek** means 'little pretty thing, jewel'.

Tegwal m.

In the Cornwall Subsidies for 1524 a *Tegwalus servant* and *alien* is recorded as living in the Borough of **Pennrynn**/Penryn. The –us suffix is a Latinization.

Tegwynn m.

This is the Cornish version of the Welsh name Tecwyn. See also **Tegwynna**.

Tegwynna f.

A feminine form of **Tegwynn**.

Tegynn m.

Another name from **Kernewek** meaning 'trinket'.

Tekka f.

This a feminine name means in **Kernewek** means 'fairer'.

Terni m.

Little is known of this saint who has two dedications; one at **Lannaled**/St. Germans and the other at **Bre Gledh**/North Hill.

Tewdar m.

Equivalent of Welsh Tewdwr. **Tewdar** is found in the place-name Lestowder **lys** 'court' + **Tewdar**. This was also the name of the pagan king of Cornwall who chased **Meryasek** founder of Camborne's parish church. Here a torturer addresses **Tewdar** in the Cornish language play **Bywnans Meryasek**, 1504;

Heyl tevder in agis tour	**Hayl, Tewdar yn agas tour!**
Meryasek an povma dor	**Meryasek a'n pow ma dour**
Galles ny ny wothen ken	**galles; ni ny wodhen ken.**
In trefov hag in gonyov	**Yn trevow hag yn goenyow**
Ny ren welas sur heb wov	**ni re'n hwilas sur, heb wow.**
Annotho covs ny wor den	**Anodho kows ny woer den.**

Hail, Tewdar in your tower! / Meryasek from this country quite / Has gone ; we know not otherwise. / In villages and on downs / We have looked for him surely, without a lie. / No one has word of him.

Tewynn f.

A name in **Kernewek** meaning 'dune' and related to the dialect 'towan' – sand dune.

Tiek m.

This name in **Kernewek** means 'farmer' and in the Cornwall Subsidies of 1545 is recorded as a Christian name; *Teacke Denys* of **Kammbronn**/Camborne. The name is also a family-name; Tyack, found in West Cornwall.

Tirek m.

In the Cornwall Subsidies for 1524 a *Tirack Nicoll* is recorded as living in **Egloswenron**/Wendron. The name may mean 'of the land'.

Tirvab m.

A bardic name that means 'son of the soil'. See **Tirvyrgh**.

Tirvyrgh f.

A name constructed on the lines of the above and meaning 'daughter of the soil'. See **Tirvab**.

Tomkyn m.

In the Cornwall Military Survey of 1522 there is a *Tomkyn Trevyssa* of **Porthia**/St. Ives.

Tomm m.

Short Cornish version of **Tommos** like Welsh Twm and English Tom.

Tommos m.

Equivalent of English Thomas and Welsh Tomos. See also **Tomm**.

Tommi m.

A Cornish equivalent of English Tommy.

Tregeredh f.

This name in **Kernewek** means 'compassion'.

Tremor m.

The Cornwall Subsidies of 1524 record a *Tremor Trern* of **Sen Pawl**/Paul parish. **Tremor** was classed as an 'alien' and **tremor** in **Kernewek** means 'overseas' so this may well be a Cornish construct. See also **Tremora**.

Tremora f.

A Cornish feminine form of the above name.

Tressa m. or f.

This name would be very appropriate for a third born child.

Trevesik m.

This was a bardic name and in **Kernewek** means 'countryman'.

Trifina m.

A Cornish equivalent for the Breton Trifina. In a song by **Brenda Wooton** there is a **Trifina Trenerry** who was 'as brown as a berry'.

Tristan m.

The most common Cornish male name. The Breton version is also Tristan. **Tristan** and **Ysult** were lovers who fled from King **Mark**. The name is derived OB and OW and is found in the place-name Tredruston.

Troenek m. or f.

Formed from **troen** 'nose' and **–ek** 'abounding in' and meaning 'nosey'. This is the name of our cat as she has a pale patch on her nose and is **troenek**.

Troeth m.

In the Arthurian triad of *Kulhogh and Olwen,* he was the great boar chased by **Arthur**. **Troeth** ran all the way to the tip of Cornwall and instead of being captured, vanished into the sea.

Truedh m.

This name in modern **Kernewek** means 'compassionate'.

Tryek m.

In the Cornwall Subsidies for 1545 a *Tryack Bonall* is recorded as living in **Kammbronn**/Camborne. This name looks Cornish as it has the **–ek** suffix which became –ack. See **Tiek**.

Tudan m.

This name is from OB and found in the place-name Tredidon.

Tudes m.

According to Gover this name is from OW and found in the place-name Nantithet.

Tudi m.

He was a friend of **Briek** and went to Brittany. **Tudi** has his church at **Eglostudi**/St. Tudy, near **Bosvenegh**/Bodmin. The Breton form is also Tudi. His feast day is on 11th May. See also **Uda**.

Tusega f.

A feminine form of the name below.

Tusek m.

A name from OB and found in the place-name Tredethick. See also **Tusega**.

Tuswal m.

This name is from OB and OW and found in the place-name Tresluswall – the well known roundabout near **Aberfal**/Falmouth. **Tuswal** has the meaning 'people powerful'. In the Cornwall Military Survey of 1522 there is a *Tudwall servanat of Harre* in the parish of **Lannanta**/Lelant.

Tybbow m.

The Cornwall Subsidies record this name as *Tybbow Bryton, Alien* of **Sen Germogh**/Germoe Parish in 1543. This name may therefore be Breton rather than Cornish.

Tygri m.

This name in **Kernewek** means 'kestrel' and has been used as a bardic name.

Uda m.

A form of **Tudi**. See also **Tudi**.

Udhno m.

This is the second half of the name Perranuthno and has the meaning 'familiar lord'.

Udi m.

Bice says that this 'was not uncommon as a 16th century Cornish Christian name' and in the Cornwall Military Survey of 1522 there is a *Udy Richard*. See also **Ewdi**.

Udyn m.

In the Cornwall Military Survey of 1522 there are three servants in **Eglosveryan**/St. Buryan Parish called *Udin*. They are listed as "Aliens born in Brittany under the obeisance of the King of France". There is also a *Udin Michell* of **Lannanta**/Lelant. *Udin* appears to be a name brought to Cornwall from Britanny.

Ughella f.

This feminine name in **Kernewek** means 'higher, more noble'.

Ughelor f.

From **Gerlyver Meur** this name in **Kernewek** means 'noble'.

Uni m.

He is patron of **Rysrudh**/Redruth and **Lannanta**/Lelant. His feast day is 1ˢᵗ February.

Unndeg f.

This is the Cornish version of the Welsh name Undeg and means 'fair, beautiful one'.

Uryn m.

In the Cornwall Military Survey of 1522 there is an *Urin Smyth* of **Porthia**/St. Ives and an *Urin Trevythyk* of **Hellys**/Helston. There is also an *Uryn* servant of *James Raw* of **Sen Germogh**/Germoe. This is a real name, I'm not taking the p***!

Ustega f.

A Cornish feminine form of the name below.

Ustek m.

From OW and found in the place-name Bosistow. Also in the Cornwall Military Survey of 1522 there is an *Ustak Herry* recorded as a tinner of **Lannyust**/St. Just in Penwith. See also **Ustega**.

Uthen m.

In the Cornwall Subsidies for 1543 an *Uthen Bryton* is recorded as living in **Lannaghevran**/St. Keverne.

Uther m.

In the Arthurian triads he is said to be the father of **Arthur**.

Uvel m.

He was a Breton missionary whose name is remembered at St. Eval, the RAF aerodrome in North Cornwall.

Uvelder m.

This name in **Kernewek** means 'humility'.

Uvella f.

A modern name from **Kernewek** meaning 'humblest'.

Uyon m.

This strange name is from OW and found in the place-name Bojowan.

Veronika f.

This is the Cornish equivalent to the Breton Veronika, French Véronique and English Veronica.

Vip m. or f.

The name survives as the village of **Sen Vip**/St. Veep, near **Fowydh**/Fowey.

Vyghan m.

Equivalent of English Vaughan or Welsh Fychan and means 'little'. In the Cornwall Military Survey of 1522 there is a *Hoskyn Vyghan and a Peter Vighan*. This shows that the name in mutated form was used a family-name and probably was then used as a Christian name. See also **Vyghana**.

Vyghana f.

A Cornish feminine form of the above name.

Wella m.

Equivalent to English William, Will, Willy, Bill and Billy. **Wella Rowe** was a 17th century Cornish speaker who translated parts of the Bible into **Kernewek**. **Wella Brown** is the Secretary of **Kesva an Taves Kernewek**/The Cornish Language Board.

Yago m.

Equivalent of English James and Welsh Iago. This name is found in the place-names Treago and Trago – yes the chain of bargain super stores! See also **Jago**.

Yakob m.

Cornish version of the biblical name Jacob.

Yernenn m.

This name is found in the place-name Treyarnon.

Yestin m.

He was son of **Gerens** and the name was found in the Bodmin Manumissions.

Yethel m.

According to Bice this name has the meaning 'generous lord'.

Yorwerth m.

Cornish equivalent of English Edward, Ed and Eddy and also Welsh Iorwerth. See also **Jorwerth**.

Yosep m.

Equivalent of English Joseph, Jo and Joey as well as Welsh Iago.

Yow m.

This would make a great name for a boy born on **Dy'Yow** 'Thursday'. See also **Yowa**.

Yowa f.

This is a feminine form of the above name.

Yowann m.

Cornish equivalent of English John, Welsh Ieuan and Breton Yann. See **Jowann**.

Yowannet f.

This is a feminine version of **Jowann**. See also **Jowannet**.

Yowav m.

This name is from OW and found in the place-name Bodieve. See **Jowav**.

Ystli m. or f.

This mysterious name is found with **Iann** 'holy enclosure' in the Cornish form of Gulval ie **Lannystli**, near **Pennsans**/Penzance.

Ythgans m.

This name comes from both OB and OC and means 'white, splendid lord'. See also **Ythgansa**.

Ythgansa f.

A Cornish feminine form of the above name.

Yudans m.

From OB and found in the place-name Trythance. See also **Judans**.

Yudek m.

This name is from OB and found in the place-name Trethick. See also **Judek**.

Yudel m.

More pioneer farmers with a Breton name who founded Bodithiel, Trethill and Truthall. See also **Judel**.

Yudreth m.

This name is from OB and found in the place-name Trehudreth. See also **Judreth**.

Yudno m.
From both OB and OW and found in the Cornish place-name Trudnoe. See also **Judno**.

Yudwal m.
This name is from OB and OW and found in the place-name Nansidwell. My great grandfather came from Nansidwell and was gored to death by a bull. See also **Judwal**.

Yungi m.
This name is from OB and found in the place-name Lesingey. See also **Jungi**.

Yunhern m.
A name that may be found in the place-name Rejame. See also **Junhern**.

Yunwal m.
From OB and found in the place-name Laninwell. See also **Junwal**.

Yunwyth m.
This name is found in the place-name Trenwith. See also **Junwyth**.

Yust m.
His name is remembered at **Lannyust**/St. Just in Penwith and **Lannsiek**/St. Just in Roseland. See also **Just**.

Ywin m.
In **Kernewek** this means 'yew' and since the best bows are made from this tree and Cornish archers were very much respected and feared in the Middle Ages, **Ywin** is a strong powerful name. See also **Ywina**.

Ywina f.
A Cornish feminine form of the above name.

Nebes Henwyn Avel Henwyn Sowsnek/
Some Common Equivalents To English Names

Name	Kernewek	Derivasion
Alan	Alan	Celtic 'rock'
Albert	Albers	Germanic 'noble, bright'
Alice	Alis	Norman French of 'Adelaide'
Andrew	Androw	Greek 'warrior'
Anne, Ann	Anna	Hebrew 'favoured'
Arthur	Arthur	Celtic 'bear like'
Bernard	Bernes	Germanic 'bear brave'
Betty	Beti	Hebrew 'God is my oath'
Blanche	Gwynna	French 'blonde'
Christopher	Kytto	Greek 'Christ to bear'
Claire, Clare	Klara	Latin 'famous'
David, Dave	Davydh	Hebrew 'darling'
Dennis	Denys	Greek 'devotee of Dionysos'
Denise	Denysa	Greek 'devotee of Dionysos'
Dick, Dicky	Hykk	Germanic 'power brave'
Edward, Eddy	Jorwerth	Germanic 'fortune guard'
Elizabeth, Liz	Eppow	Hebrew 'God is my oath'
Eric	Erik	Scandinavian 'forever power'
Erica	Eriga	Feminine form of 'Eric'
Gareth	Gareth	Celtic 'gentle'
Gavin	Gawen	Celtic 'hawk white'
Geoffrey, Geof	Jeffra	Germanic 'territory pledge'
George	Jori, Yori	Greek 'farmer'
Georgina	Joria	Greek 'farmer'
Gilbert	Jilberth	Germanic 'pledge bright'
Guy	Gwion	Germanic 'wide'
Harry	Harri	Germanic 'home power'

Helen, Lena	Elena	Greek 'sun beam'
Henry	Henna	Germanic 'home power'
Honor	Enor	Latin 'honour'
Humphrey	Humfra	Germanic 'bearcub piece'
Isabell	Esbell	Spanish version of 'Elizabeth'
Jack, Jacky	Jakka	Germanic diminutive of 'John'
James	Jago	Latin of Hebrew version 'Jacob'
Jane, Jayne	Jenna	French feminine version of 'John'
Jenifer	Gwynniver	Celtic 'white phantom'
John, Jonny, etc.	Jowann	Hebew 'God is gracious'
Joseph, Joe	Josep	Hebew '(God) shall add (another)'
Josephine, Josey	Jowsepa	French feminine of 'Joseph'
Joy	Lowena	Latin 'joyful'
June	Metheven	English 'June month'
Katherine, Kathy	Kattell	Greek 'pure'
Luke	Luk	Latin 'light'
Malcolm	Kolomm	Celtic 'follower of St. Colum'
Mark, Markus	Margh	Latin of unknown derivation
Mary	Maria	Latin 'star of the sea'
Matthew, Matt	Mathi	Hebrew 'gift of God'
May	Me	Short form of Margaret or Mary
Michael, Mike	Mighal	Hebrew 'who is like God?'
Michelle, Michaela	Mighala	Germanic feminine of 'Michael'
Molly, Moll	Mali	Pet form of 'Mary'
Nicholas	Nykklys	Greek 'victory people'
Nick, Nicky	Nykka	Short form of 'Nicholas'
Noel	Nadelik	Latin 'birthday of the Lord'
Owen	Owynn	Celtic 'borne of yew'
Patricia, Pat	Padrega	Latin feminine form of 'Patrick'
Patrick, Paddy	Padrek	Celtic of unknown derivation
Paul	Pawl, Pol	Latin 'small'

Paula	Pawla	Feminine form of 'Paul'
Pauline	Polin	French feminine of 'Paul'
Peter, Pete	Peder	Greek 'stone or rock'
Philip, Phil	Fylip	Greek 'love horse'
Richard	Hykka	Germanic 'power hardy'
Robert, Bob	Robas	Germanic 'fame bright'
Roger	Rojer	Germanic 'fame spear'
Rose, Rosey	Rosenn	Latin 'rose the flower'
Simon	Symon	Hebrew 'hearkening'
Stefan	Stephen	Greek 'garland or crown'
Stephanie	Stefana	Feminine form of 'Stephen'
Sue	Siw	Short form of 'Susan'
Susan	Siwsann	Hebrew 'shoshan lily'
Thomas	Tommas	Greek 'twin'
Tom	Tomm	Short form of 'Thomas'
Tristan	Tristan	Celtic 'sad one'
Veronica	Veronika	Latin 'true image'
Victor, Vic	Gwyther	Latin 'conqueror'
Victoria, Vicky	Budheka	Feminine of 'Victor'
William, Bill	Wella	Germanic 'wish helmet'

Sesonyow/Seasons

Spring	**gwenton**	summer	**hav**
Autumn	**kynyav**	winter	**gwav**

Misyow/Months

Strictly speaking January, February, March etc. in **Kernewek** are **mis-Genver, mis-Hwevrer, mis-Meurth etc.** (the **Kernewek** for month being **mis**) dropping the **mis-** prefix gives us twelve good names.

January	**Genver**	February	**Hwevrer**
March	**Meurth**	April	**Ebryl**
May	**Me**	June	**Metheven**
July	**Gortheren**	August	**Est**
September	**Gwynngala**	October	**Hedra**
November	**Du**	December	**Kevardhu**

Dydhyow/Days

Strictly speaking Monday, Tuesday, Wednesday etc. in **Kernewek** are **dy'Lun, dy'Meurth, dy'Mergher** (the **Kernewek** for day being **dydh**, the **dy'** is an abbreviation of **dydh**) dropping the **dy'** prefix gives us seven good personal names.

Sunday	**Sul**	Monday	**Lun**
Tuesday	**Meurth**	Wednesday	**Mergher**
Thursday	**Yow**	Friday	**Gwener**
Saturday	**Sadorn**		

Dydhyow Goel/Feast Days

The modern day celebrations of St. Piran's Day are not confined to the 5th of March. The pilgrimage across the dunes at **Porthpyran**/Perranporth takes place on the nearest Sunday. The **keskerdh Sen Pyran**/St. Piran's Day parade in **Truru**/Truro takes place on the nearest weekday in order to let schools participate. The thirty or so events are spread out over a week so anyone born at 'Pirantide' could take the name **Pyran** therefore names could be bestowed on someone born on or around the following dates.

Dydh/Day	**Tyller**/Place	**Gwel yn-dann**/See under
6th January	**Eglosvelyan**/Mullion	**Melyan**
13th January	**Sen Alan**/St. Allen	**Alan**
13th January	**Sen Erbin**/St. Erbyn	**Erbin**
18th January	**Sen Day**/St. Day	**Day**
19th January	**Sen Branwaldader**/St. Breward	**Branwalader**
1st February	**Rysrudh**/Redrudh	**Uni**
2nd February	**Sen Fiek**/Feock	**Fiek**
3rd February	**Porthia**/St. Ives	**Ia**
8th February	**Lanndogho**/St. Kew	**Kywa**
22nd February	**Porthleven**	**Elwynn**
1st March	**Lanndhewi**/Davidstow	**Dewi**
3rd March	**Gwynnwallow**/Gunwalloe	**Gwynnwalow**
5th March	**Porthpyran**/Perranporth	**Pyran**
7th March	**Sen Enosek**/St. Enodoc	**Enosek**
8th March	**Porthsenan**/Sennen Cove	**Senan**
9th March	**Lanngostenin**/Constantine	**Kostentin**
23rd March	**Sen Gwynnyer**/Gwinear	**Gwynnyer**
4th April	**Sen Niet**/St. Neot	**Gweryr**
7th April	**Bosvenegh**/Bodmin	**Goran**
24th April	**Sen Iv**/St. Ive	**Iv**
27th April	**Eglosenoder**/Sen Enoder	**Enoder**
29th April	**Sen Endelyn**/St. Endellion	**Endelyn**

Dydh/Day	Tyller/Place	Gwel yn-dann/See under
1st May	**Sen Briek**/St. Breock	**Briek**
1st May	**Eglostedha**/St. Teath	**Tedha**
2nd May	**Sen Gennys**/St. Gennys	**Gennys**
3rd May	**Sen Glevyas**/St. Gluvias	**Glevyas**
5th May	**Lannhydrek**/Lanhydrock	**Hydrek**
11th May	**Eglostudi**/St. Tudy	**Tudi**
17th May	**Eglosvadern**/Madron	**Madern**
20th May	**Sen Kolan**/Colan	**Kolan**
4th June	**Eglosvrega**/Breage	**Brega**
4th June	**Eglosveryan**/St. Buryan	**Beryan**
4th June	**Lannwedhenek**/Padstow	**Petrek**
12th June	**Sen Pawl**/Paul	**Pawl**
15th June	**Alternonn**/Altarnun	**Nonn**
17th June	**Sen Nyghtan**/St. Nectan	**Nyghtan**
21st June	**Sen Mewan**/St. Mewan	**Mewan**
24th June	**Sen Germogh**/Germoe	**Germogh**
25th June	**Sen Selevan**/St. Levan	**Seleven**
28th June	**Sen Ostell**/St. Austell	**Ostell**
1st July	**Lannwenepa**/Gwennap	**Gwenepa**
1st July	**Sen Vip**/St. Veep	**Vip**
5th July	**Lannbroboes**/Probus	**Proboes**
7th July	**Sen Meren**/St. Merryn	**Meren**
8th July	**Lannvorwenna**/Morwenstow	**Morwenna**
23rd July	**Golgh a-ves**/Washaway	**Konan**
28th July	**Goelnans**/Golant	**Samson**
29th July	**Logsulyen**/Luxulyan	**Sulyen**
31st July	**Sen Niet**/St. Neot	**Niet**
4th August	**Sen Sydhni**/Sithney	**Sydhni**
30th August	**Ruan**	**Ruan**
24th September	**Sen Mowgan**/St. Mawgan	**Mowgan**
24th September	**Mownan**/Mawnan	**Mownan**
25th September	**Fowydh**/Fowey	**Fimbarrus**

Dydh/Day	Tyller/Place	Gwel yn-dann/See under
1st October	**Ponsnowydh**/Mylor	**Meler**
3rd October	**Sen Ke**/Kea	**Ke**
8th October	**Sen Keyna**/St.Keyne	**Keyna**
18th October	**Morval**	**Gwenna**
31st October	**Lannudhno**/St. Erth	**Erk**
4th November	**Sen Kleder**/St. Clether	**Kleder**
4th November	**Sen Kler**/St. Cleer	**Kler**
6th November	**Sen Gwynnek**/St. Winnow	**Gwynnek**
6th November	**Sen Pynnek**/St. Pinnock	**Pynnek**
13th November	**Sen Kolomma**/St. Columb	**Kolomma**
18th November	**Lannvowsedh**/St. Mawes	**Mowsedh**
18th November	**Lannaghevran**/St. Keverne	**Aghevran**
18th November	**Sen Mabon**/St. Mabyn	**Mabon**
20th November	**Sen Eval**/St. Eval	**Eval**
24th November	**Sen Menvra**/St. Minver	**Menvra**
8th December	**Plywvudhek**/Budock	**Budhek**
12th December	**Egloskri**/Cury	**Korentin**
14th December	**Sen Felek**/Phillack	**Piala**

This list contains only a selected number of Cornish saints. Perhaps someone born in or around April 23rd could be named **Jori** the Cornish equivalent for George.

ΠEBES LYVROW/ SELECT BIBLIOGRAPHY

1. *Names for the Cornish*, Christopher Bice, Dyllansow Truan, **Truru**/Truro, **Kernow**/Cornwall, 2nd Edition 1984.

2. *The Place-names of Cornwall*, J.E.B. Gover, Unpublished script, R.I.C. **Truru**/Truro, **Kernow**/Cornwall, 1948.

3. *A Popular Dictionary of Cornish Place-names*, O.J. Padel, Alison Hodge, **Pennsans**/Penzance, **Kernow**/Cornwall, 1988.

4. *1,000 Cornish Place-names Explained*, Julyan Holmes, Dyllansow Truran, **Rysrudh**/Redruth, **Kernow**/Cornwall, 2nd Edition, 1999.

5. *Henwyn Tylleryow Yn Kernow*, **Kowethas an Yeth Kernewek**/Cornish Language Fellowship, Ken George, Pol Hodge, Julyan Holmes & Graham Sandercock, **Lyskerrys**/Liskeard, **Kernow**/Cornwall, 1995.

6. *The Cornish Saints*, Peter Berresford Ellis, Tor Mark Press, **Pennrynn**/Penryn, **Kernow**/Cornwall, 1992.

7. *The Saints of Cornwall*, Catherine Rachel John, Lodenek Press & Dyllansow Truran, **Lannwedhenek**/Padstow, **Kernow**/Cornwall, 1981.

8. *Enwau Cymreag I Blant/Welsh Names For Children*, Heini Gruffudd, Y Lolfa, Talybont, **Kembra**/Wales, 2nd Edition 1980.

9. *Grand Choix de Prénoms Bretons*, Gwennole Le Menn, Coop Breizh, Spezet, **Breten Vyghan**/Brittany, 1990.

10. *Les Prénoms de Bretagne*, Yvon Autret, Editions Ouest-France [sic], Roazon/Rennes, **Breten Vyghan**/Brittany, 1996.

11. *Tous Les Prénoms Bretons,* Alain Stéphan, Editions Jean-Paul Gisserot, **Pow Frynk**/France, 1996.

12. *Scottish First Names*, George Mackay, Waverley Books, New Lanark, **Alban**/Scotand, 1998.

13. *Irish First Names*, Julia Cresswell, HarperCollins, Glasgow, **Alban**/Scotland, 1996.

14. *The Oxford Minidictionary of First Names*, Oxford University Press, Oxford, **Pow Sows**/England, 1986

15. *Gerlyver Kernewek Kemmyn, Gerlyver Meur*, Dr. Ken George, **Kesva an Taves Kernewek**/Cornish Language Board, **Bosprenn, Kernow**/Cornwall, 1993.

16. *The New Standard Cornish Dictionary, An Gerlyver Kres*, Dr. Ken George, **Kesva an Taves Kernewek**/Cornish Language Board, **Bosprenn, Kernow**/Cornwall, 1998.

17. *A Grammar of Modern Cornish*, Wella Brown, **Kesva an Taves Kernewek**/Cornish Language Board, **Essa**/Saltash, **Kernow**/Cornwall, 2nd Edition, 1993.

18. *King Arthur's Avalon*, Geoffrey Ashe, Collins, **Loundres**/London, **Pow Sows**/England, 1957.

19. *The Making of Modern Europe*, Robert Bartlett, Princeton University Press, New Jersey, **Statys Unys**/United States, 1993.

20. *Cornwall Military Survey 1522*, T.L. Stoate. Bristol, **Pow Sows**/England, 1985.

21. *Cornwall Subsidies in the Reign of Henry VIII*, T. L. Stoate, Bristol, **Pow Sows**/England, 1985.

22. *Bywnans Meryasek*, edited by Whitley Stokes, **Kernewek Dre Lyther**, Sutton Coldfield, **Pow Sows**/England, 1996.

23. *The Tregear Homilies*, Ray Edwards, **Kernewek Dre Lyther**, Sutton Coldfield, **Pow Sows**/England, 1994.

24. *Origo Mundi,* Ray Edwards, **Kernewek Dre Lyther**, Sutton Coldfield, **Pow Sows**/England, 1998.

25. *Passio Christi*, Ray Edwards, **Kernewek Dre Lyther**, Sutton Coldfield, **Pow Sows**/England, 1999.

26. *An Sowter*, R.K.R. Syed, **Kesva an Taves Kernewek**/Cornish Language Board, Cheltenham, **Pow Sows**/England, 1997.

Gras Dhe/Thanks To

Cliff Stephens who prompted me to write this book after many a beery hour at the **Gorsedh** or **Lowender Pyran** – I can't remember which.

Ken George for his great efforts in keeping me on the phonemic straight and narrow and checking the worst excesses of my appalling English spelling!

June Luxton who can take a myth, legend or simply a name and bring it to life before your very eyes with her drawings.

Chris Bowden for advice on layout, printing and photography.

Kesva an Taves Kernewek/Cornish Language Board for help with ISBN and publishing.

And to **Jane**, my wife, for proof-reading, kerbing the excesses of my ranting when I've been **ughel** and encouraging me to get on with it when I've been **isel.**

For furthur explanation on any matters concerning the Cornish language contact;

Kesva an Taves Kernewek
Jori Ansell,
65 Treveglos/65 Churchtown,
Sen Gwynnyer/Gwinear,
Heyl/Hayle
Kernow

(01736) 850878
jori-ansell@talk21.com

Fentenwynn Cultural Services;
Fentenwynn,
Bre Wartha/Top Hill,
Fordh Ponsmeur/Grampound Road,
Truru/Truro,
Kernow.

(01726) 882681
fentenwynn@hotmail.com